"I have no doubt that *Lenten Healing* will be of great help to people desiring freedom and restoration in Jesus Christ. The meditations are inspiring, deep, and healing. This book will lead you to encounter God's personal love for you and give you the courage to face and let go of what holds you back from living the abundant life in him."

Sr. Miriam James Heidland, S.O.L.T.
Catholic speaker and author of *Loved As I Am*

"If you are anything like me you have dealt with some type of repetitive sin or behavior, something you desired to be free from. Ken Kniepmann in *Lenten Healing* unpacks the roots of sin, the power of grace, and the reality of freedom we have in Christ. This is a devotional we should all journey through."

Paul George
Catholic speaker and author of *Rethink Happiness*

"Ken Kniepmann does an amazing job of leading us on a guided Lenten retreat into the 'super-structure' of sin—the interior tangled web of past wounds and the complicated response of our hearts toward sin as a medication for all that mess—with illuminating force, accessing God's grace and healing all along the way!"

Jim Beckman
Executive director of evangelization and catechesis
Archdiocese of Oklahoma City

"The integration of prayer, emotional healing, and growth in Christian virtue in *Lenten Healing* is both brilliant and profound. If you want freedom from the deeper places of your sin and from the hurts and wounds that drive sin, read this book and allow Jesus to heal you and set you free."

Rev. Mathias Thelen, S.T.L.
Pastoral administrator of St. Patrick Parish
Brighton, Michigan

"Ken Kniepmann presents a simple and helpful understanding of the human person and the effects of sin and grace in the human heart. Artfully using scripture, insightful reflections, and healing prayers, *Lenten Healing* provides a practical way to have a deepening prayer experience amidst the regular demands of daily life. Anyone who embarks on this forty-day journey in faith can expect to be led by the Holy Spirit and grow in self-knowledge, healing, and with God's grace, freedom from sin."

Most Rev. Andrew Cozzens
Auxiliary Bishop of St. Paul and Minneapolis

"*Lenten Healing* expands our concept of Lenten fasting from obligation to awakening. Through this approach to the Lenten disciplines of fasting and prayer, Ken Kniepmann offers readers an opportunity to deepen our vision of what it means to be free, whole, and loved by God."

Audrey Assad
Catholic singer, songwriter, and musician

D0062483

LENTEN HEALING

40 Days to Set You Free from Sin

KEN KNIEPMANN

Foreword by Bob Schuchts

Ave Maria Press · AVE · Notre Dame, Indiana

Foreword © 2017 by Bob Schuchts

_____

Founded in 1865, Ave Maria Press is a ministry of the United States Province of Holy Cross.

www.avemariapress.com

Paperback: ISBN-13 978-1-59471-795-6

E-book: ISBN-13 978-1-59471-796-3

Cover image © iStockphoto.com.

Cover and text design by Brianna Dombo.

Printed and bound in the United States of America.

Library of Congress Cataloging-in-Publication Data
Names: Kniepmann, Ken, author.
Title: Lenten healing : 40 days to set you free from sin / Ken Kniepmann.
Description: Notre Dame, IN : Ave Maria Press, 2018.
Identifiers: LCCN 2017040023 | ISBN 9781594717956 (pbk.)
Subjects: LCSH: Lent--Prayers and devotions. | Grace (Theology)--Prayers and devotions. | Catholic Church--Prayers and devotions.
Classification: LCC BX2170.L4 K55 2018 | DDC 242/.34--dc23
LC record available at https://lccn.loc.gov/2017040023

Contents

Foreword

I believe the practical program for spiritual healing contained in this book will be life-changing for all who engage in it with an open heart. It is a perfect resource for Lent, since it is a forty-day spiritual journey designed to facilitate deep and lasting transformation. But its application goes well beyond Lent. I have no doubt that this short book will be of great value to every person in every season of life and throughout the liturgical year, because the spiritual-growth process it promotes is universal.

Fasting and prayer are ancient spiritual practices that predate Christ and have been an integral part of the Church since its very beginning. These disciplines, while highlighted during the season of Lent, are meant to be practiced every day of our lives, because they increase the capacity of our hearts to receive a greater measure of the Holy Spirit.

What is especially unique about this book is the kind of fasting and prayer it promotes. It calls us to shed the false attachments of our deadly sins and debilitating wounds so that we can enter more fully into the joy of the risen Christ. One of my favorite quotes from the *Catechism of the Catholic Church* speaks to this: "The desire and work of the Holy Spirit in the heart of the Church is that we may live the life of the Risen Christ" (*CCC*, 1091). This book will allow you to partner with the Holy Spirit to release those barriers and restrictions that keep your heart bound and cut off from Christ's resurrected life.

As you work your way through the different sections of this book, renouncing the Seven Deadly Sins and praying through the wounds that undergird them, you will find yourself growing in joy and freedom and with an increased capacity to give and receive love.

I have known the author, Ken Kniepmann, for more than ten years. We are friends and coworkers, serving together at the John Paul II Healing Center. I can testify that Ken has lived and breathed the material that he writes about in this book. He speaks from years of personal experience as well as many hours assisting others on their path to healing and transformation.

I am confident that this spiritual program will serve as a good preparation and follow-up for all who attend our conferences at the John Paul II Healing Center. But even more than that, I am excited for the whole Church to discover the riches of grace and wisdom that Ken lays out in these pages.

If you desire greater freedom and happiness in your life but haven't known how to find them, this book will be a trustworthy guide. Ask the Holy Spirit to assist you as you work through the various sections. I believe you will be amazed at what the Lord can do in forty days.

Bob Schuchts
Founder of the John Paul II Healing Center
and author of *Be Healed* and *Be Transformed*

Preface

This book, as with so many of the great experiences in my life, had a modest and unintended beginning. While I grew up in a predominantly Catholic Midwest environment, living in the Deep South over the last decade has exposed me to a much less insular world of faith, one in which I encounter the broader Body of Christ on a daily basis. Despite the sometimes wide theological differences between denominations, I'm constantly amazed at the ways in which God speaks to all the Christian faithful and how often he plants seeds in places that might seem unlikely.

A similar origin motivated this book. I had read a work by a woman whom I can best describe as a Pentecostal–Evangelical kingdom minister. In it, author Rebecca King told the amazing story of how God had supernaturally rescued her from a life that was on a path to tragedy. A profound encounter with God brought her deep healing and restoration, completely changing the trajectory of her life.

Several months later, I found myself cruising King's resource table at a local conference. On the table was a three-ring binder—the kind you buy for your kids' classwork—filled with sheets in page protectors. The title of this rather modest-looking resource caught my attention: *40 Day Soul Fast.* I opened it to the table of contents and realized that the author was on to something. It was a guided "fast" from the things that bring true hardship into our lives—sin, hurt, negative emotions, and self-defeating beliefs. I immediately saw the applicability of this idea to our ministry work at the John Paul II Healing Center.

This seemed to be an inspired concept, although it lacked the richness and order that are offered by Catholic understanding. Drawing on the Church's deep knowledge, I began to organize this idea around two central themes: the Seven Deadly Sins and the things within us that cause us to sin, which I will refer to as the Seven Deadly Wounds. Dr. Bob Schuchts, founder of the John Paul II Center, was instrumental in helping me structure these reflections in a way that was easy to understand and follow. It was at Bob's suggestion that I approached Ave Maria Press about publishing this book.

I also owe a debt of gratitude to my editor, Kristi McDonald, at Ave Maria Press. Her suggestions in the early part of the process resulted in the inclusion of the Sunday reflections and the additional prayer reflection on Fridays. I believe this book can help you identify and rid yourself of destructive thoughts, beliefs, emotions, and behaviors. After all, it makes a lot of sense to fast from things that are *not* good for us. This book provides a practical way to work on the negative influences that attempt to afflict us and will help us come to a deeper relationship with God and experience more joy in life!

Introduction

You want to destroy yourself? Cling to
your warring emotions; they will devour
you. You want to save yourself? Hook
those passions onto the infinite purposes
of God and you will find yourself elevat-
ed, transfigured, enlightened. Pressed
in the direction of sanctity, you will save
your life.
—Bishop Robert Barron

Through this observation, Bishop Barron shares with us
two important truths. First, clinging to sin is as deadly
and dangerous to us in this world as it is in the next. It
leads us to destruction, not life. Second, sin is connected
to things inside us. With great insight, Bishop Barron
calls them "warring emotions." How often do we find
ourselves at war with ourselves? We feel unable to keep
ourselves from doing things we'd rather not do.

A simple illustration can help explain this predicament. I first heard this analogy from Fr. Mark Toups, and its imagery will give you a reference for the entire book. Imagine that you have an apple tree growing in your yard. Every year, it produces a fresh crop of apples. It doesn't produce cherries or peaches or pears. Why? Because, obviously, it is an apple tree. Now, assume that the apples on that tree are your sins. You pick the apples off the tree through repentance, confession, and effort. You really want different fruit in your life, something other than apples. But frustratingly, you always seem to end up with more apples.

It's easy to see that we keep getting apples because that is what grows on apple trees. If we want peaches, we need a peach tree. If we want cherries, we need a cherry tree. If we want to change the fruit, we need to change the *root*. Applying this analogy to our sin, we can say that sin is a fruit. So if our sin is a fruit, what are the root and tree it grows on? These are the "warring emotions" Bishop Barron refers to. In this book, we'll take a deeper look at the roots of our sin. We will look at how our sin is actually rooted in our thoughts, our beliefs, and our emotions (feelings).

Sin is the fruit of thoughts, beliefs, and emotions (think of these as the trunk of the tree) that are rooted in hurt and pain. As we are bumped and bruised by life, we begin to believe things about ourselves, others, and the world that are not true. Instead of being in harmony with heaven, our "inside life" of thoughts, beliefs, and emotions is in harmony with the world and the enemy.

If you've ever experienced despair, fear, shame, powerlessness, or hopelessness, you've experienced a reaction to being hurt. Despair might come out as a belief—"It will never get better." Powerlessness might come out as a thought—"Everybody is taking advantage of me." These are not God's truths, but when we accept them as if they are true, we will live according to them. Our own thoughts and beliefs can actually resist God. They hem us in and lead us to behave in ways that are destructive to ourselves, others, and our relationship with God.

Now let's turn to the subject of fasting for a moment and how we're going to approach that practice in this book. As you probably know, fasting is an ancient tradition of the Christian church. We often fast from things we enjoy, things that are pretty benign such as chocolate or other favorite food. It's much harder to fast from the things that protect our hurt and that actually shackle us to mediocrity and misery. All of us have these things in our lives. They keep us from experiencing the fullness of God's mercy and purpose for us. In the pages of this book, I'll help you identify some of the shackles in your life as we carefully examine the many different sources and manifestations of sinfulness.

Our fast is organized around four Sevens: the Seven Deadly Sins, Seven Contrary Virtues, Seven Deadly Wounds, and Seven Signs of Healing. Each week, we will contemplate one of the sins and its corresponding virtue, wound, and sign of healing. For example, in the first week we will look at Sloth (sin), Diligence (virtue), Confusion (wound), and Understanding (sign of healing). Each week, the deadly sin or deadly wound will have additional days of reflection. In week one, as we look at the wound of confusion, we will explore some specific aspects of it, like double-mindedness and false-burden bearing.

Don't be constrained by the framework of this reflection. While wounds and sins tend to find natural connections, you may experience them outside this particular framework. For example, you might experience the wound of powerlessness as a root for the sin of anger instead of lust. Pay attention to your own thoughts, feelings, and beliefs. The following graphic illustrates the potential connections between sins and wounds. The solid lines indicate the most common connections, and the framework for this book. The dotted lines represent the possible other connections you might make between sins and wounds.

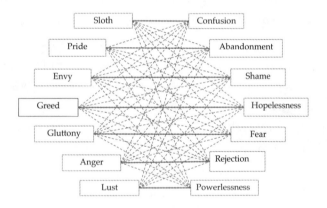

The Seven Deadly Sins and the Seven Contrary Virtues have a deep history within the Church. Much has been written and taught about them, while the Seven Deadly Wounds and the Seven Signs of Healing are drawn primarily from the decades of work done by Bob Schuchts. (You can dig deeply into the topic of spiritual healing with Bob Schuchts's book *Be Healed: A Guide to Encountering the Powerful Love of Jesus in Your Life*.) As the weekly reflections unfold, you will begin to see the connections between sin, wounds, virtue, and healing—both in reason and within your own interior experience.

As you go through each meditation, pay attention to your thoughts, your feelings, and your beliefs. The enemy will often prompt us in one of these three areas to give us a shove from life to death. He invites us to accept these negative and faulty internal experiences. Don't be surprised if this fast reveals sins and wounds that are new to you. Some of our wounds, and the patterns of thought, belief, and emotion accompanying them, are as old as we are and so deeply ingrained in us that we can hardly see them.

When you reach the Friday reflection, you will find an additional prayer experience. This is a simple prayer based on St. Ignatius's work. It is a manner of praying that allows God to speak to you around the week's topic. This prayer style may be easy for you or quite new and unfamiliar. Even if it seems fruitless at first, I encourage you to keep with it. Trust that God will work through it.

Each Sunday is a *feast* day. It is a celebration, embracing God's grace in the virtue and healing of the week. Living in the reality of God's goodness and healing is important for us. Thanksgiving is one of the most effective ways to embrace this reality.

This fast is for you if you want freedom from the deeper places of your sin, and the hurts and wounds that drive sin. I encourage you to give this fast adequate time in your schedule. Take time to pray, to allow the Holy Spirit and Jesus to speak to your heart. As you read the daily reflection, give it time to penetrate your mind and your heart. Pay attention to words or phrases that excite, agitate, or disturb your emotions. Linger over the scripture passages and quotes from the saints. Give yourself time to answer the reflection questions, and say the closing prayer aloud, slowly, and with emphasis. Allow God to reveal himself to you. Let him show you your sin and hurts. Invite him into your pain. Let him speak to you in it. Wherever you find pain, rest assured that you will also find freedom and mercy nearby in the person of Jesus Christ.

WEEK 1. SLOTH AND CONFUSION

Day 1: Ash Wednesday

Today, I choose to fast from the sin of *sloth*.

There might not be a better place to start a Lenten fast than with the sin of sloth. We often think of sloth as being lazy, but the meaning of this sin is much deeper. St. Thomas Aquinas called sloth a sadness or "sorrow for spiritual good" (*Summa* II:II:35). Sloth is much more about what goes on *inside of us* than about our lack of action. There are two easy measures for this sin in our lives. First: balance. Do you have a good balance between work, family, leisure, and prayer? Too much here and not enough there is an indicator of sloth. Second: effort. If you lack passion or enthusiasm, can't get started, can't finish, can't persevere in hardship, or become distracted or diverted, sloth is a likely culprit. For example, sloth will probably want you to quit this fast at some point. But persevere and make firm your resolve by working slowly through the following meditation.

Pause to hear God speak . . .

"The sluggard buries a hand in the dish, too weary
to lift it to the mouth. In their own eyes sluggards are
wiser than seven who answer with good judgment."

—Proverbs 26:15–16

"We earnestly desire each of you to demonstrate the
same eagerness for the fulfillment of hope until the end,
so that you may not become sluggish, but imitators of
those who, through faith and patience, are inheriting
the promises."

—Hebrews 6:11–12

Take time to ask yourself . . . *'21 giving myself a*
free
What is out of balance in my life? *– scheduling* *pass*
When do I become easily diverted or distracted from *'20*
things that are important? *– overwhelmed, desiring leisure*
'21 when I'm tired, when Usdi is
napping

Pray slowly . . .

Heavenly Father,

In the name of our Lord Jesus Christ, I renounce
sloth and repent all the ways in which I have operated in it. I reject every form of sloth in my life. I ask
you, Father, to forgive me, and I forgive myself for my

slothful heart and actions. Holy Spirit, fill me with enthusiasm, passion, and eagerness, and make me aware of any slothful thoughts, feelings, or actions. Amen.

Day 2: Thursday

Today, I choose to fast from the wound of *confusion*.

The story of Adam and Eve gives us the perfect analogy to understand our sin. In Genesis, the fruit that Adam and Eve eat represents sin. If our own sin is fruit, it also grows on a tree, and that tree has roots. Our sin is a reaction to something that happens deeper inside of us—at our roots. These roots are made up of our experiences, emotions, beliefs, and thoughts that are separate from God's love and care for us. Let's take a moment to zero in on this idea by looking at the wound of confusion.

Using our tree analogy, we can see that confusion is a primary *root* of the sin of sloth. In other words, sloth is our reaction to being confused. If you've ever been sure you should make a right turn while driving, only to find out you really should have turned left, that is confusion. Confusion happens inside us—it is a disorientation of our mind, emotion, or heart. It might feel to you like a thick fog in your head. It might also feel like a rapid back-and-forth in your thoughts. We just can't figure out the right direction or right thing to do. Confusion will keep us from making a decision, or lead us toward a bad decision. Confusion is at the root, but sloth is the fruit. Working with the reflection below, take a few moments to ponder the presence of confusion in your life.

Pause to hear God speak . . .

"He is not the God of disorder [confusion] but of peace."
— 1 Corinthians 14:33

"But if any of you lacks wisdom, he should ask God who gives to all generously and ungrudgingly, and he will be given it."

— James 1:5

Take time to ask yourself . . .

What type of thoughts and feelings tend to confuse me? How do I react when I experience confusion?

Pray slowly . . .

Heavenly Father,

In the name of our Lord Jesus Christ, I renounce confusion and repent all the ways in which I have sinned because of it, particularly the ways in which I have rejected your wisdom and peace. I reject every form of confusion in my life. I renounce any lies that I have come to believe, including lies such as "I don't know what to do," "I'll make a mistake," or "I don't know where to turn." Send your Holy Spirit to heal, restore, and transform me. Amen.

Day 3: Friday

Today, I choose to fast from the wound of *double-mindedness*.

Wherever you are right now, take a few seconds to look directly in front of you. Now, while still looking straight ahead, turn around and look behind you. It's impossible! You cannot look ahead and behind at the same time. Yet this is what it feels like to be double-minded. The original Greek meaning of the term is "two selves" or "two souls." You might feel *in* and *out*, *wanting* and *not wanting*, *committed* and then *hesitating*, or wanting *one thing* and then *another*. This is an emotionally exhausting kind of confusion. We are in conflict with ourselves and unable to choose a direction. We feel unsteady. While the scriptures encourage us to be steadfast, resolute, and to set our "face like flint" (Is 50:7), we are unable to pick a direction. Double-mindedness leaves us vulnerable to doubt and undercuts our faith. Now that we know how to recognize double-mindedness in our lives, let's take some time to reflect on how we can combat it.

Pause to hear God speak . . .

"That person must not suppose that he will receive any-thing from the Lord, since he is a man of two minds, unstable in all his ways."

—James 1:7–8

"So submit yourselves to God. Resist the devil, and he will flee from you. Draw near to God, and he will draw near to you. Cleanse your hands, you sinners, and puri-fy your hearts, you of two minds."

—James 4:7–8

Take time to ask yourself . . .

When do I experience restlessness and conflict inside myself?

How do I deal with being double-minded?

Pray slowly . . .

Heavenly Father,

In the name of our Lord Jesus Christ, I renounce double-mindedness and repent all the ways in which

I have sinned because of it, particularly the ways in which I have not drawn closer to you, Father, and have been unstable in my love for you. I reject double-mindedness in every area of my life. I renounce any lies that I have come to believe, including lies such as "I can't make up my mind" or "It won't work out anyway." I renounce any companion emotions such as confusion. Send your Holy Spirit to speak the truth to my heart that I may have the "mind of Christ" (1 Cor 2:16). Amen.

Prayer Meditation on Sloth and Confusion

Invite God to be with you now.

Father, send your Holy Spirit to minister to the deep places of my heart during these moments of quiet reflection. Allow my own hurts, pains, and wounds to be drawn into the very wounds of Jesus that we reflect upon today. Jesus, you showed us that the way to the resurrected life is through death to the bondage of the world. Allow me to receive you, Jesus, during this time of prayer, to know that you desire to heal the pain and hurts of my heart. Lord Jesus, I trust you to guide me during this time with you. Come, Holy Spirit.

1. Quietly reflect . . .

Think of a time that you've experienced deep feelings of slothfulness or confusion. Specifically name the emotions that you are experiencing. *During those times: depression, anxiety, apathy, anger, hurt, self-pity, self-centeredness, pain*

2. Pray . . .

Lord, I trust you to care for my heart in this time. Please show me any places within my life where these emotions are rooted (perhaps a memory).

What did God show you?

3. Write down the negative things you believe about yourself, about God, and about others in the emotions and memory. God doesn't care, I'm worthless,

4. If the Lord showed a memory to you, pray . . .

Lord, I thank you for exposing this painful experience and memory to me. Please reveal to me anything that you would like me to know.

In our painful memories, we often believe that God was not present to us in those difficult experiences. If we prayerfully invite the Lord into those memories, he will often reveal himself to us. As you do this, you might see an image in your mind, hear him speak to you, or just have a *sense* of him, which might be as simple as experiencing the truth come against the wrong belief in your heart, which is at the source of your pain. This simple contemplative/imaginative prayer can help us to know God in a more personal and intimate way.

If you don't experience anything in this exercise, that is OK too. Often, wounds and sins "buddy up," which makes them stubborn. If that is the case, don't be discouraged! Just allow the Lord to work in his time.

5. Pray . . .

Lord, I thank you for healing grace. I trust that you speak to the deepest places of my heart, even if I don't sense it. I thank you for instilling in me the truth of your deep and extravagant love for me. I thank you, as I pray right now, for restoration of every area of my life that has been stolen or compromised by sin and wounds. I bless your name!

Day 4: Saturday

Today, I choose to fast from the wound of *false-burden bearing*.

If you're a parent, at some point you've likely been more concerned about your child being ready for a big test than they were. You might have hovered over them or badgered them to study and prepare. Your concern and personal investment were far greater than theirs. This is an example of false-burden bearing. We might justify it as *mercy* or *diligence,* but we are really taking on the cares, concerns, and responsibilities that rightly belong to someone else. This wound can masquerade as compassion, but it's really a form of confusion: I cannot tell the difference between what is *mine* and what is *yours*.

At deeper levels of hurt, abuse victims will blame themselves for what was done to them, or family members will blame themselves for a loved one's suicide. False-burden bearing often connects to other faulty beliefs and emotions related to guilt and shame. It is a form of codependency, where we believe that we are somehow responsible for the outcomes of other people's decisions, and we will do everything in our power to *save* the other person. Let's work through this a little bit as we reflect on the following passages, questions, and prayers.

Pause to hear God speak . . .

"Each will bear his own load."

—Galatians 6:5

"Come to me, all you who labor and are burdened, and I will give you rest. Take my yoke upon you and learn from me, for I am meek and humble of heart; and you will find rest for yourselves. For my yoke is easy, and my burden light."

—Matthew 11:28–30

Take time to ask yourself . . .

How do I try to fix or save others?
What burden do I carry that doesn't belong to me?

Pray slowly . . .

Heavenly Father,

In the name of our Lord Jesus Christ, I renounce false-burden bearing and repent all the ways in which I have sinned because of it, particularly in not loving authentically and by getting in the way of your work. I reject all forms of false-burden bearing in my life. I renounce any lies that I have come to believe, including lies such as "I can fix them" or "It's my responsibility." I renounce any companion emotions such as confusion and double-mindedness. Send your Holy Spirit to speak the truth to my heart that I may have the "mind of Christ" (1 Cor 2:16). Amen.

Feast Day: Sunday

Today, I choose to feast on _diligence_ and _understanding_.

Diligence is the virtue that replaces sloth, and understanding removes confusion. Our diligence is motivated by desire and passion for the things of God. We are excited to move forward and ready to get under way. We know where we are going and we want to get there.

In today's gospel reading, Jesus goes into the wilderness. After forty days, he must have been tired, hungry, and thirsty. Because of _understanding_, Jesus was _diligent_ in his resistance to Satan's temptations. Jesus understood who he was and why he was here. This allowed him to stand firm in the face of temptation and resist the shortcuts to comfort and power offered by the enemy.

Try to get to Mass a little early today. Settle into your seat, and offer your week to God. In your mind, place it on the altar and prepare your heart for the gifts of the liturgy. As you pray for the Lord's mercy during the Penitential Act, allow your heart to release sloth and confusion.

Embrace the good news (gospel) of diligence and understanding that is available to you, and celebrate your restoration and healing in the Eucharist.

Remember that Lent is the preparation for resurrection, for freedom, for joy.

Pause to hear God speak . . .

"We are the Easter people and hallelujah is our song."

—St. John Paul II

"Therefore, my beloved brothers, be firm, steadfast, always fully devoted to the work of the Lord, knowing that in the Lord your labor is not in vain."

—1 Corinthians 15:58

"The beginning of wisdom is: get wisdom; whatever else you get, get understanding."

—Proverbs 4:7

Take time to ask yourself . . .

What is my purpose or mission?
How does God see me?

Pray slowly . . .

Heavenly Father,

In the name of our Lord Jesus Christ, and by the power of the Holy Spirit, I accept the gifts of <u>diligence</u> and <u>understanding</u> in my life. I accept my identity as the beloved child of a gracious Father God. I thank you for my life's purpose and the strength to fulfill it. I accept your healing grace. Amen.

WEEK 2. PRIDE AND ABANDONMENT

Day 5: Monday

Today, I choose to fast from the sin of *pride*.

Wouldn't it be great to wake up every morning and feel the love of God penetrating every part of you, knowing that he loves you to the core of your being? I don't know about you, but that's not exactly how it works for me. Instead, it's all too easy to feel alone. Rather than feeling like a beloved child, we feel like orphans who have to make our way in a hostile world. Our response to these deep feelings can be both powerful and destructive because of how quickly we replace the confidence that we long to receive from God with a shallow confidence in ourselves. Our thoughts, beliefs, and emotions tell us, "You don't need anybody," "You don't need help," and "You can do this on your own." Instead of depending on God, we depend on ourselves and our own strength.

St. Thomas Aquinas calls pride "the love of one's own excellence" (*Summa*, II:II:162). The loud, bombastic egotist is an obvious caricature of a prideful person, but pride is equally at home inside our quiet piety, false humility, and self-reliance. You can see pretty quickly why St. Gregory the Great, and St. Thomas Aquinas after him, considered pride to be the queen of all vices.

Let's take a few minutes to see the ways in which we let pride into our lives as we try to save ourselves instead of trusting ourselves to God.

Pause to hear God speak . . .

"To believe one does not need counsel is great pride."

—St. Basil the Great

"He has shown might with his arm, dispersed the arrogant of mind and heart. He has thrown down the rulers from their thrones but lifted up the lowly."

—Luke 1:51–52

Take time to ask yourself . . .

In what ways am I prideful?

How does my pride affect my view of God?

Pray slowly . . .

Heavenly Father,

   In the name of our Lord Jesus Christ, I renounce pride and repent all the ways in which I have sinned because of it. I reject every form of pride in my life. I ask you, Father, to forgive me, and I forgive myself for my prideful heart and actions. Holy Spirit, make me aware of any prideful thoughts, feelings, and actions. Amen.

Day 6: Tuesday

Today, I choose to fast from the sin of *self-reliance*.

One of the many faces of pride is self-reliance. We rely on ourselves, acting and believing that God is not to be trusted with a part of our lives. We might trust God in many areas of our lives, but there is usually at least one area where we rely on ourselves.

Do you trust your finances to God? How about your relationships? Your marriage? Your children? We prize self-reliance in Western culture, and it is deeply ingrained in the American ethic. In reality, self-sufficiency is a godless reliance on ourselves and a self-neglect of our hearts and souls. Our reliance on ourselves is a refusal of the grace and power of God. We live as if we know ourselves and our needs better than God. We live as if we are alone. When we live in self-reliance, we really say to God and others, "I don't need you." It is a lonely and depressing way to live that is doomed to ultimate failure. Sooner or later, we will be confronted by a situation that we cannot solve. As you continue this reflection, try to examine every area of your life for self-reliance.

Pause to hear God speak . . .

"Not that of ourselves we are qualified to take credit for anything as coming from us; rather, our qualification comes from God."

—2 Corinthians 3:5

"But [the Lord] said to me, 'My grace is sufficient for you, for power is made perfect in weakness.' I will rather boast most gladly of my weaknesses, in order that the power of Christ may dwell with me."

—2 Corinthians 12:9

Take time to ask yourself . . .

Where in my life do I strive for independence? When do I make decisions and act before seeking God? Check in with your work life, family life, and personal activities. What am I afraid will happen if I become dependent on God in this area of my life?

Pray slowly . . .

Heavenly Father,

In the name of our Lord Jesus Christ, I renounce self-reliance and repent all the ways I have acted out of it. I reject every form of self-reliance and self-sufficiency in my life. I ask you, Father, to forgive me, and I forgive myself for relying on my own strength and knowledge, and all the times that doing so has tempted me to sin. Holy Spirit, make me aware of any self-reliant thoughts, feelings, and actions. Amen.

Day 7: Wednesday

Today, I choose to fast from the sin of *self-promotion*.

If you're really honest with yourself, you've probably thought or said, "When will it be my turn? I've waited long enough. I've been faithful. I've done all the right things." We become agitated in the *waiting* of life, believing that nobody is looking out for us. When we don't get the things we think we deserve, our frustration can lead us to arrange events and relationships that will promote ourselves. Often, that frustration exposes things we believe about God, even though they are not true. We might believe that he *isn't good* because he won't give us what we desire or that he's *not capable* because he isn't giving us what we deserve.

Self-promotion may be at work in you if you find yourself seeking recognition at the expense of others, boasting, or striving for admiration through your actions. You can even be tempted to self-promotion around something good like a vocational call, but doing so will simply cause you to move ahead of God's timing. God often allows us to glimpse his plans for us through our own desires, which are meant to encourage us. But God rarely gives us the detailed roadmap. Our impatience with God in the journey can lead us to move ourselves forward instead of trusting God's timing. Now that we can identify this particular form of pride, let's reflect on eliminating it from our lives.

Pause to hear God speak . . .

"We put pride into everything like salt. We like to see that our good works are known. If our virtues are seen, we are pleased; if our faults are perceived, we are sad."

—St. John Vianney

"For everyone who exalts himself will be humbled, but the one who humbles himself will be exalted."

—Luke 14:11

Take time to ask yourself . . .

What am I seeking when I attempt to promote myself? What in me wants to be admired and respected by others? Why?

Pray slowly . . .

Heavenly Father,

In the name of our Lord Jesus Christ, I renounce self-promotion and repent all the ways in which I have acted out of it. I reject every form of self-promotion in my life. I ask you, Father, to forgive me, and I forgive myself for my self-promotion, and all the times that it has tempted me to sin. Holy Spirit, make me aware of any self-promoting thoughts, feelings, and actions. Amen.

Day 8: Thursday

Today, I choose to fast from the sin of *narcissism*.

It may be an extension cord, headphone cable, or string of Christmas lights. We put it away neatly, and pull it out to find a hopelessly knotted mess. This image helps describe the inner workings of narcissism. In this type of pride, our uniqueness to our heavenly Father becomes tangled up with the *littleness* of our humanity before him. We confuse our God-given *specialness* with an illusion of *greatness*. We are so confident of our own specialness that we think others cannot relate to us.

Here are some key questions you might consider to help yourself identify any narcissistic tendencies: Do you think that nobody really understands you? Do you think that others can't possibly comprehend your inner workings? Is it hard to receive compassion from others when you believe that they really can't understand? Take some time to really think about your answers to those questions because they can be indicators of different forms of narcissism in your life. Narcissistic beliefs often make us expect everything and everyone to order themselves to our pain, perceptions, and emotions. Let's dig a little deeper with the meditation below to check in with our own narcissism.

Pause to hear God speak . . .

"Because we are proud; we should like to be the sole possessors . . . of all the world. We hate our equals, because they are our equals; our inferiors, from the fear that they may equal us; our superiors, because they are above us."

—St. John Vianney

"[Love] is not rude, it does not seek its own interests, it is not quick-tempered, it does not brood over injury."

—1 Corinthians 13:5

Take time to ask yourself . . .

Where in my life do I believe I am more special than others?

In what ways do I believe that nobody really understands me because nobody else is like me?

Pray slowly . . .

Heavenly Father,

In the name of our Lord Jesus Christ, I renounce narcissism and repent all the ways in which I have acted out of it. I reject every form of narcissism in my life. I ask you, Father, to forgive me, and I forgive myself for my narcissistic tendencies, and all the times they have tempted me to sin. Holy Spirit, make me aware of any narcissistic thoughts, feelings, and actions. Amen.

Day 9: Friday

Today, I choose to fast from the wound of *abandonment*.

It might not be immediately apparent, but if you take a few moments to think about it, the connection between pride and abandonment becomes obvious. Most of us have had an experience of being lost as a child, maybe on an outing with family members. If a memory popped into your head while you were reading this, it probably has some powerful emotions associated with it. You likely felt *alone*, *isolated*, *unprotected*, or *uncovered*. You might have experienced abandonment in your life through your parents' divorce or a death. Even innocent experiences, like being lost, can leave us with a deep emotional hurt of abandonment.

We can begin to expose and uproot this wound by examining the thoughts, beliefs, and emotions in our hearts. If you are hyperloyal, or require it of others, you might be guarding an abandonment hurt by requiring allegiance or duty. Have you ever felt that? Perhaps you've thought, "In the end, I'll always be alone," "It will always be up to me," or "Nobody will be there to protect me." Let's take some time during the reflection below to allow God to speak to and minister to this wound.

Pause to hear God speak . . .

"[God] has said, 'I will never forsake you or abandon you.'"

—Hebrews 13:5

"The LORD will not forsake his people, nor abandon his inheritance."

—Psalm 94:14

Take time to ask yourself . . .

What are some of my memories or thoughts around abandonment?

What do I believe about myself and my life as a result of those memories or thoughts?

Pray slowly . . .

Heavenly Father,

In the name of our Lord Jesus Christ, I renounce abandonment and repent all the ways in which I have sinned because of it. I reject abandonment in every area of my life. I renounce any lies that I have come to believe, including lies such as "I am all alone," "I am on my own," or "Nobody cares about me." Send your Holy Spirit to heal, restore, and transform me. I belong to you. I am loved by you. I am chosen by you. I am known to you. Amen.

Prayer Meditation on Pride and Abandonment

Invite God to be with you now.

Father, send your Holy Spirit to minister to the deep places of my heart during these moments of quiet reflection. Allow my own hurts, pains, and wounds to be drawn into the very wounds of Jesus that we reflect upon today. Jesus, you showed us that the way to the resurrected life is through death to the bondage of the world. Allow me to receive you, Jesus, during this time of prayer, to know that you desire to heal the pain and hurts of my heart. Lord Jesus, I trust you to guide me during this time with you. Come, Holy Spirit.

1. Quietly reflect . . .

Think of a time that you've experienced deep feelings of being alone or abandoned. Specifically name the emotions that you are experiencing.

2. Pray . . .

Lord, I trust you to care for my heart in this time. Please show me any places within my life where these emotions are rooted (perhaps a memory).

What did God show you?

3. Write down the negative things you believe about yourself, about God, and about others in the emotions and memory.

4. If the Lord showed a memory to you, pray . . .

Lord, I thank you for exposing this painful experience and memory to me. Please reveal to me anything that you would like me to know.

In our painful memories, we often believe that God was not present to us in those difficult experiences. If we prayerfully invite the Lord into those memories, he will often reveal himself to us. As you do this, you might see an image in your mind, hear him speak to you, or just have a *sense* of him, which might be as simple as experiencing the truth come against the wrong belief in your heart, which is at the source of your pain. This simple contemplative/imaginative prayer can help us to know God in a more personal and intimate way.

If you don't experience anything in this exercise, that is OK too. Often, wounds and sins "buddy up," which makes them stubborn. If that is the case, don't be discouraged! Just allow the Lord to work in his time.

5. Pray . . .

Lord, I thank you for healing grace. I trust that you speak to the deepest places of my heart, even if I don't sense it. I thank you for instilling in me the truth of your deep and extravagant love for me. I thank you, as I pray right now, for restoration of every area of my life that has been stolen or compromised by sin and wounds. I bless your name!

Day 10: Saturday

Today, I choose to fast from the wound of *loneliness*.

You might be old enough to remember the 1960s hit song "One Is the Loneliest Number." Even pop culture knows that loneliness is broken and incomplete. We are meant to live in communion and relationship with others and with God. Yet we've all been lonely at times. If you've experienced some of the sins and wounds we have discussed this week, perhaps the sin of self-reliance or the wound of abandonment, your loneliness may feel like a dark, empty hole.

In our abandonment hurt, we protect ourselves from others by relying only on ourselves. We end up alone and lonely, which further feeds our feelings of being abandoned. You might feel completely alone and isolated, even when you are with loved ones. The sense of being alone can be overwhelming and incapacitating. As you reflect on this, you might find that your loneliness also connects with wounds of rejection and fear.

Pay attention to the root memories, thoughts, beliefs, and emotions that authored and now trigger these hard feelings. Let's listen to what the Holy Spirit is trying to tell us about the deepest parts of our hearts.

Pause to hear God speak . . .

"And behold, I am with you always, until the end of the age."

—Matthew 28:20

"Father of the fatherless, defender of widows—God in his holy abode, God gives a home to the forsaken, who leads prisoners out to prosperity."

—Psalm 68:6–7

Take time to ask yourself . . .

In what types of situations do I normally feel lonely? What memories do I have (perhaps memories of self-reliance or abandonment) that seem to trigger feelings of loneliness?

Pray slowly . . .

Heavenly Father,

In the name of our Lord Jesus Christ, I renounce loneliness and repent all the ways in which I have sinned because of it. I reject loneliness in every area of my life. I renounce any lies that I have come to believe, including lies such as "I am all alone," "Nobody will save me," "Nobody really cares," or "Nobody will notice if I'm not here." Send your Holy Spirit to speak the truth to my heart that I am loved, cared for, and am not alone. Amen.

Feast Day: Sunday

Today, I choose to feast on *humility* and *connectedness*.

Humility is the virtue that replaces pride, and connectedness heals the wound of abandonment. Remember, we come to humility by knowing who we are in God's eyes, rather than our own eyes or the eyes of others. In today's gospel, Jesus, Peter, James, and John go up a mountain. Three of the most stunning supernatural events recorded in all of scripture are manifested before the disciples' eyes. First, Jesus appears in his glorified state, with his face shining like the sun. Then, Moses and Elijah show up for a chat with Jesus. Finally, heaven opens up, and the Father blesses Jesus' identity.
How did Jesus react to all of this? First, he told the apostles to fear not. Second, he told them not to tell anybody what happened.

Jesus knew who he was—no need to brag. The Father blessed him in love—no need to feel alone. Our humble hearts, connected to God, recognize our smallness before him while experiencing his immense, intimate, and personal love for each of us as unique and unrepeatable.

Try to get to Mass a little early today. Settle into your seat, and offer your week to God. In your mind, place it on the altar and prepare your heart for the gifts of the liturgy. As you pray for the Lord's mercy during the Penitential Act, allow your heart to release pride and abandonment.

Embrace the good news (gospel) of humility and connectedness that is available to you, and celebrate your restoration and healing in the Eucharist.

Remember that Lent is the preparation for resurrection, for freedom, for joy.

Pause to hear God speak . . .

"We are the Easter people and hallelujah is our song."
—St. John Paul II

"Do you wish to be great? Then begin by being. Do you desire to construct a vast and lofty fabric? Think first about the foundations of humility. The higher your structure is to be, the deeper must be its foundation."
—St. Augustine

"For by the grace given to me I tell everyone among you not to think of himself more highly than one ought to think, but to think soberly, each according to the measure of faith that God has apportioned."

—Romans 12:3

Take time to ask yourself . . .

What do I believe God thinks about me?

How do I connect with God in my daily life?

Pray slowly . . .

Heavenly Father,

In the name of our Lord Jesus Christ, and by the power of the Holy Spirit, I accept the gifts of humility and connectedness in my life. I accept my identity as the beloved son/daughter of a gracious Father God. I thank you for my life's purpose and the strength to fulfill it. I accept your healing grace. Amen.

WEEK 3. ENVY AND SHAME

Day 11: Monday

Today, I choose to fast from the sin of *envy*.

If we are honest with ourselves, celebrating the good fortune of those around us can often leave us feeling a little empty on the inside. It might begin as a simple thought: "Why them and not me?" Before long, we are comparing ourselves to others in a way that breeds sorrow and sadness. We think, "Why do they have that and I don't? I'm more deserving. I'm smarter, better, and harder working." The hallmarks of our envy are a *lack of kindness, mercy, and love*. We end up being judgmental and unkind to others.

Envy makes it easy for us to believe that we are left out or deprived. We rejoice in the misfortune of others, and are even willing to tear them down. This in turn renders us dangerously vulnerable to deep feelings of sadness and sorrow.

Pause to hear God speak . . .

"A tranquil mind gives life to the body, but jealousy rots the bones."

—Proverbs 14:30

"Do nothing out of selfishness or out of vainglory; rather, humbly regard others as more important than yourselves, each looking out not for his own interests, but everyone for those of others."

—Philippians 2:3–4

Take time to ask yourself . . .

What types of people and occasions make me envious? How do I feel when I believe I deserve more than I have?

Pray slowly . . .

Heavenly Father,

In the name of our Lord Jesus Christ, I renounce envy and repent all the ways in which I have acted out of it. I reject every form of envy in my life. I ask you, Father, to forgive me, and I forgive myself for my envious heart and actions. Holy Spirit, fill me with joy, humility, and love of others. Make me aware of any envious thoughts, feelings, or actions. Amen.

Day 12: Tuesday

Today, I choose to fast from the sin of *judgment*.

Many men I know bear deep animosity toward their fathers. These feelings usually stem from the idea that their fathers were in some way cold, distant, hard, absent, mean, or even cruel. These men have been hurt by their fathers, and they judged their fathers for it. But by looking deeper into their fathers' own history, many of these men found compassion for the same father they hated.

It's pretty easy to judge the hearts and motivations of those around us. We look at their actions and decide (make a judgment) about them or their motives. Many of the men I mentioned eventually understood the deep pain and hurt their own fathers had endured, and they were moved from judgment to compassion. Their fathers' own pain had been the root of sinful behavior that, in turn, hurt their sons. Judgment is a sin that unfortunately encourages us to hang on to unforgiveness in our lives.

Pause to hear God speak . . .

"Therefore, you are without excuse, every one of you who passes judgment. For by the standard by which you judge another you condemn yourself, since you, the judge, do the very same things."

—Romans 2:1

"Stop judging by appearances, but judge justly."

—John 7:24

Take time to ask yourself . . .

Who in my life have I judged and why?
What do I believe about their motives toward me?

Pray slowly . . .

Heavenly Father,

In the name of our Lord Jesus Christ, I renounce judgment and repent all the ways in which I have acted out of it. I reject every form of judgment in my life. I ask you, Father, to forgive me. I forgive myself for my judgments. Holy Spirit, make me aware of any judgmental thoughts, feelings, and actions. Amen.

Day 13: Wednesday

Today, I choose to fast from the wound of *shame*.

What do you believe God sees when he looks at you? Are you a beloved, amazing, beautiful masterpiece? Or are you a disappointment? Shame is a deep wound against our identity that tells us we are *inferior* in some way. It motivates us to hide in order to cover up our failings and inadequacies. For many of us, shame comes at an early age. Shame may occur when our parents or caretakers don't honor and respect us as they should. In other cases, though, we carry shame as a judgment against ourselves. We become so familiar with it that we don't even recognize it in our lives. We learn to hide all the things that we don't like about ourselves.

The voice of shame may sound to you like, "You're inadequate," "You're a failure," or "You're undesirable." Shame is so powerful a wound that abuse victims will often blame themselves for being abused. It is also one of the wounds that keeps us from the sacrament of

Reconciliation. Let's pay close attention to our emotions and beliefs as we continue the reflection below.

Pause to hear God speak . . .

"Do not fear, you shall not be put to shame; do not be discouraged, you shall not be disgraced."

—Isaiah 54:4

"Keeping our eyes fixed on Jesus, the leader and perfecter of faith. For the sake of the joy that lay before him he endured the cross, despising its shame, and has taken his seat at the right of the throne of God."

—Hebrews 12:2

Take time to ask yourself . . .

Which events in my life am I ashamed of?
What types of experiences lead me to feel shame?

Pray slowly . . .

Heavenly Father,

In the name of our Lord Jesus Christ, I renounce shame and repent all the ways in which I have sinned because of it, particularly the ways in which I have not lived into the fullness of who you have made me. I reject every form of shame in my life. I renounce any lies that I have come to believe, including lies such as "I am no good," "I am dirty," "I am ugly," or "I am inadequate." I renounce any companion emotions such as unworthiness, self-condemnation, and guilt. Send your Holy Spirit to speak the truth to my heart that I am loved, cared for, and am not alone. Amen.

Day 14: Thursday

Today, I choose to fast from the wound of *unworthiness*.

We've all felt unworthy, sometimes in a good way that checks narcissism and pride. But more often, unworthiness is a nagging kind of shame that sabotages our own good. As soon as we begin to dream a little, to become passionate about something, we hear that voice inside of our hearts. It says, "I'm not good enough," "I'll just screw up anyway," or "I could never do that; who am I?"

When we allow unworthiness to take root in our lives, we shrink back and lose courage when life requires some level of risk, whether emotional, spiritual, or physical. We become complacent and mediocre, and believe that not even God can produce fruit from our lives. If you feel like a failure, dishonorable, undeserving, or unqualified, you are experiencing unworthiness. Let's dig deep during the reflection below to uncover the unworthiness that limits our lives.

Pause to hear God speak . . .

"You formed my inmost being; you knit me in my mother's womb. I praise you, because I am wonderfully made; wonderful are your works!"

—Psalm 139:13–14

"For I know well the plans I have in mind for you—oracle of the LORD—plans for your welfare and not for woe, so as to give you a future of hope."

—Jeremiah 29:11

Take time to ask yourself . . .

What kinds of experiences lead me to feeling unworthy? When I feel unworthy, which old memories or thoughts come to mind?

Pray slowly . . .

Heavenly Father,

In the name of our Lord Jesus Christ, I renounce unworthiness and repent all the ways in which I have sinned because of it, particularly the ways in which I have not answered your call in my life. I reject every form of unworthiness in my life. I renounce any lies that I have come to believe, including lies such as "I am not good enough," "I am not qualified," or "I'm not worth it." I renounce any companion emotions such as shame, self-condemnation, and guilt. Send your Holy Spirit to speak the truth to my heart that I am worthy. Amen.

Day 15: Friday

Today, I choose to fast from the wound of *condemnation*.

What kind of image comes to mind when you picture God? Is he a loving Father? Or is he an angry tyrant? If there is any area where you see God as an angry judge, condemnation probably has a hold on your life. Simply, condemnation is the judgment we put upon ourselves; it is self-imposed. We pronounce ourselves as unfit or judge ourselves as guilty.

As we do so, we place ourselves in a kind of spiritual captivity that chains us to a place under ourselves instead of under God. Instead of experiencing the freedom of Jesus' Resurrection and the gifts of God's grace and forgiveness, we're bound to our own poor opinion of our self. Spend a few quiet moments with our opening question before continuing on with the reflection below: How do you imagine God?

Pause to hear God speak . . .

"For freedom Christ set us free; so stand firm and do
not submit again to the yoke of slavery [condemnation]."

—Galatians 5:1

"Who will bring a charge against God's chosen ones? It
is God who acquits us. Who will condemn? It is Christ
[Jesus] who died, rather, was raised, who also is at the
right hand of God, who indeed intercedes for us."

—Romans 8:33–34

Take time to ask yourself . . .

How do I condemn myself?

Whose voice do I hear within my heart when I experience feelings of condemnation?

Pray slowly . . .

Heavenly Father,

In the name of our Lord Jesus Christ, I renounce
condemnation and repent all the ways in which I have
sinned because of it, particularly the ways in which
I have rejected your forgiveness and grace. I reject
condemnation and break the chains of self-imposed
punishment over my heart, mind, will, and spirit. I

renounce any lies that I have come to believe, including lies such as "I can never be forgiven" or "God is not big enough for my pain, sin, or hurt." I renounce any companion emotions such as shame, unworthiness, and guilt. Send your Holy Spirit to speak the truth to my heart that I am free. Amen.

Prayer Meditation on Envy and Shame

Invite God to be with you now.

Father, send your Holy Spirit to minister to the deep places of my heart during these moments of quiet reflection. Allow my own hurts, pains, and wounds to be drawn into the very wounds of Jesus that we reflect upon today. Jesus, you showed us that the way to the resurrected life is through death to the bondage of the world. Allow me to receive you, Jesus, during this time of prayer, to know that you desire to heal the pain and hurts of my heart. Lord Jesus, I trust you to guide me during this time with you. Come, Holy Spirit.

1. Quietly reflect . . .

Think of a time that you've experienced deep feelings of envy or shame. Specifically name the emotions that you are experiencing.

2. Pray . . .

Lord, I trust you to care for my heart in this time. Please show me any places within my life where these emotions are rooted (perhaps a memory).

What did God show you?

3. Write down the negative things you believe about yourself, about God, and about others in the emotions and memory.

4. If the Lord showed a memory to you, pray . . .

Lord, I thank you for exposing this painful experience and memory to me. Please reveal to me anything that you would like me to know.

In our painful memories, we often believe that God was not present to us in those difficult experiences. If we prayerfully invite the Lord into those memories, he will often reveal himself to us. As you do this, you might see an image in your mind, hear him speak to you, or just have a *sense* of him, which might be as simple as experiencing the truth come against the wrong belief in your heart, which is at the source of your pain. This simple contemplative/imaginative prayer can help us to know God in a more personal and intimate way.

If you don't experience anything in this exercise, that is OK too. Often, wounds and sins buddy up, which makes them stubborn. If that is the case, don't be discouraged! Just allow the Lord to work in his time.

5. Pray . . .

Lord, I thank you for healing grace. I trust that you speak to the deepest places of my heart, even if I don't sense it. I thank you for instilling in me the truth of your deep and extravagant love for me. I thank you, as I pray right now, for restoration of every area of my life that has been stolen or compromised by sin and wounds. I bless your name!

Day 16: Saturday

Today, I choose to fast from the wound of *guilt*.

Guilt cuts deeply into our lives in many ways that we don't realize. It's connected closely to shame, the wound that leaves us feeling inadequate and inferior. Guilt lines up our past failings against us and keeps us attached to them. Our negative, self-incriminating feelings and thoughts become the measure of our lives. Guilt would say to an all-star baseball player, "You only get a hit three out of ten times. That is a 70 percent failure rate!" When we sin and fail, remorse, not guilt, is the proper response. Remorse is a sorrow that pricks our conscience when we sin. It helps us seek mercy and forgiveness without becoming attached to our failure. After years of confessing the same sins, St. Ignatius of Loyola recognized that guilt was an impediment to a deeper relationship with God. On this last fast day of the week, let's seek God in a special way.

Pause to hear God speak . . .

"Let us approach with a sincere heart and in absolute trust, with our hearts sprinkled clean from an evil conscience and our bodies washed in pure water."

—Hebrews 10:22

"All shall know me, from least to greatest. For I will forgive their evildoing and remember their sins no more."

—Hebrews 8:11–12

Take time to ask yourself . . .

What do I feel guilty about?

When I experience guilt, what are the thoughts of self-reproach?

Pray slowly . . .

Heavenly Father,

In the name of our Lord Jesus Christ, I renounce guilt and repent all the ways in which I have sinned because of it, particularly the ways in which I have rejected your forgiveness and grace. I reject guilt in every area of my life and renounce any and all thoughts of self-reproach or self-incrimination. I renounce any lies that I have come to believe, including lies such as "I'm too far gone," "I can never recover," or "I'm a screw-up." I renounce any companion emotions such as shame, unworthiness, and condemnation. Send your Holy Spirit to speak the truth to my heart that I am free. Amen.

Feast Day: Sunday

Today, I choose to feast on _kindness_ and _worthiness_.

Kindness is the virtue that replaces envy, and worthiness heals the wound of shame. We come to kindness by knowing who we are in God's eyes, rather than through our own eyes or the eyes of others. Every third year, the gospel for today is the incredible story of Jesus' encounter with the Samaritan woman at the well (see John 4:5–42). It is a story filled with the woman's shame, guilt, and condemnation. She has been married five times and is currently living with a man outside of marriage. Because of her shame, she avoids the well in the morning when others might be there. On this particular day, Jesus meets her there. With amazing kindness and mercy, he frees her from her shame. After her encounter, she goes into the streets to preach about Jesus to anyone who will listen. She has been found to be worthy by Jesus—_and that is everything!_

Try to get to Mass a little early today. Settle into your seat, and offer your week to God. In your mind, place it on the altar and prepare your heart for the gifts of the liturgy. As you pray for the Lord's mercy during the Penitential Act, allow your heart to release envy and shame.

Embrace the good news (gospel) of kindness and worthiness that is available to you, and celebrate your restoration and healing in the Eucharist.

Remember that Lent is the preparation for resurrection, for freedom, for joy.

Pause to hear God speak . . .

"We are the Easter people and hallelujah is our song."

—St. John Paul II

"I, then, a prisoner for the Lord, urge you to live in a manner worthy of the call you have received, with all humility and gentleness, with patience, bearing with one another through love."

—Ephesians 4:1–2

Take time to ask yourself . . .

What does it mean for me to be worthy in God's eyes?

How has God shown his kindness in my life?

Pray slowly . . .

Heavenly Father,

In the name of our Lord Jesus Christ, and by the power of the Holy Spirit, I accept the gifts of kindness and worthiness in my life. I accept my identity as the beloved child of a gracious Father God. I thank you for my life's purpose and the strength to fulfill it. I accept your healing grace. Amen.

WEEK 4. GREED AND HOPELESSNESS

Day 17: Monday

Today, I choose to fast from the sin of *greed*.

For most of us, one name captures the image of greed—Scrooge. Ebenezer Scrooge, the central character in Charles Dickens's *A Christmas Carol*, shows us a lot about this deadly sin. In Scrooge, we see all the outward signs of greed—gain at the expense of others, hoarding, cheating, and miserliness. We also see how the sin of greed grows in one's thoughts, beliefs, and emotions long before it is a sin on the *outside*. Scrooge's life is anchored in a deeply held belief that there will never be enough or that he might go without. The thought that he might have little or nothing drives every decision in his life. Greed motivates us, too, to gain more and more possessions, even at the expense of love and personal relationships. In greed, we often believe deep down that our dreams, wishes, and needs won't be fulfilled. As we continue with the meditation below, let's allow God to show us where greed has a hold in our own lives.

Pause to hear God speak . . .

"The covetous are never satisfied with money, nor lovers of wealth with their gain; so this too is vanity. Where there are great riches, there are also many to devour them. Of what use are they to the owner except as a feast for the eyes alone?"

—Ecclesiastes 5:9–10

"Those who want to be rich are falling into temptation and into a trap and into many foolish and harmful desires, which plunge them into ruin and destruction. For the love of money is the root of all evils, and some people in their desire for it have strayed from the faith and have pierced themselves with many pains."

—1 Timothy 6:9–10

Take time to ask yourself . . .

Do I ever feel like I will never have enough of something? What?

In what am I willing to cut a corner to achieve an end?

Pray slowly . . .

Heavenly Father,

In the name of our Lord Jesus Christ, I renounce greed and repent all the ways in which I have operated in it. I reject every form of greed in my life. I ask you, Father, to forgive me, and I forgive myself for my greedy heart and actions. Holy Spirit, fill me with generosity and make me aware of any greedy thoughts, feelings, and actions. Amen.

Day 18: Tuesday

Today, I choose to fast from the wound of *hopelessness*.

Hope has two ingredients—the *desire* for something and the *belief* that it might happen. Whenever we feel hopeless, desire and/or belief are missing. Without desire, we simply lack enthusiasm and zeal. If you have trouble getting motivated, a lack of desire may be the issue. We will spend more time with unbelief in a future meditation, but it is at work in your life if you think the future is bleak. When we are hopeless, we often think to ourselves, "What's the point?" "It'll never change," or "It won't get any better." As we look at our lives, we find that these negative *thoughts* connect to negative *emotions* such as apathy. Go deep enough, and you might find a belief that God really doesn't care about you. Today, let's especially ask God to show us and heal us of our hopelessness.

Pause to hear God speak . . .

"Consider how he endured such opposition from sinners, in order that you may not grow weary and lose heart."

—Hebrews 12:3

"It is the LORD who goes before you; he will be with you and will never fail you or forsake you."

—Deuteronomy 31:8

Take time to ask yourself . . .

What are the things in my life that seem impossible? Why?

What are the things that make me feel enthused and motivated? Why?

Pray slowly . . .

Heavenly Father,

In the name of our Lord Jesus Christ, I renounce hopelessness and repent all the ways in which I have sinned because of it, particularly the ways in which I have despaired and given up. I reject hopelessness in every area of my life. I renounce any lies that I have come to believe, including lies such as "It will never get better," "I'll never have what I want," or "God doesn't care about the things I want." I renounce any companion emotions such as disappointment, discouragement, and worry. Send your Holy Spirit to transform my heart and mind, giving me supernatural hope. Amen.

Day 19: Wednesday

Today, I choose to fast from the wound of *disappointment*.

Each of us has been let down in life. Maybe it's been with a job, a personal relationship or something we hoped to accomplish. Disappointment is a natural emotional reaction to the things in life that don't go the way we hoped. But when disappointment becomes a way of thinking, it moves *inside* us and becomes personal. If you expect things to go wrong or to not work out, disappointment may be working in your life. Maybe you secretly wait *for the other shoe to drop,* or regularly think that good things are *too good to last.* Disappointment like this becomes a self-inflicted wound. Disappointment can also occur when we attach unrealistic expectations to a goal, believing that everything will be perfect when we reach it. Even when we attain the goal, it can't be as perfect as we imagined it. So we feel disappointed. Let's put disappointment in its place, and get it out of the areas of our lives where it doesn't belong.

Pause to hear God speak . . .

"Do not hide your face from me in the day of my distress. Turn your ear to me; when I call, answer me quickly. For my days vanish like smoke; my bones burn away as in a furnace. My heart is withered, dried up like grass."

—Psalm 102:2–5

"The LORD is close to the brokenhearted, saves those whose spirit is crushed. Many are the troubles of the righteous, but the LORD delivers him from them all."

—Psalm 34:19–20

Take time to ask yourself . . .

What in my life has been a disappointment?
How do I deal with disappointment?

Pray slowly . . .

Heavenly Father,

In the name of our Lord Jesus Christ, I renounce disappointment and repent all the ways in which I have sinned because of it, particularly the ways in which I have given up. I reject every form of disappointment in my life. I renounce any lies that I have come to believe, including lies such as "I'll never have what I want." I renounce any companion emotions such as discouragement and worry. Send your Holy Spirit to transform my heart and mind, giving me supernatural hope. Amen.

Day 20: Thursday

Today, I choose to fast from the wound of *worry*.

Imagine yourself sitting in a rocking chair, going back and forth as quickly as you can. It's just about a perfect picture of worry—lots of motion that goes nowhere. The motion that we experience in worry can be summed up by the question "What if?": "What if my car doesn't start?" "What if I mess up?" "What if nobody loves me?" Worry is a self-inflicted torment where we think about every possible *negative* outcome. A baseball player who thinks about striking out with bases loaded in the bottom of the ninth inning will not hit many game-winning home runs. He focuses so much on the negative that he is not free to *go for it.* When we worry, we wear ourselves out physically, emotionally, and spiritually. If you are anxious or uneasy and find yourself dwelling on trouble, worry is working in your life. Whether you realize it or not, you are building a mountain of negative "what ifs" and then pointing at that mountain as proof that there is no hope. As we continue today, let's reflect on ways in which we can come out of worry.

Pause to hear God speak . . .

"So humble yourselves under the mighty hand of God, that he may exalt you in due time. Cast all your worries upon him because he cares for you."

—1 Peter 5:6–7

"Have no anxiety at all, but in everything, by prayer and petition, with thanksgiving, make your requests known to God. Then the peace of God that surpasses all understanding will guard your hearts and minds in Christ Jesus."

—Philippians 4:6–7

Take time to ask yourself . . .

What do I worry about?

Why do I seem to dwell on the negative possibilities?

Pray slowly . . .

Heavenly Father,

In the name of our Lord Jesus Christ, I renounce worry and repent all the ways in which I have sinned because of it, particularly the ways in which I have focused on negative things. I reject worry in every area of my life. I renounce any lies that I have come to believe, and I renounce any companion emotions such as disappointment and hopelessness. Send your Holy Spirit to transform my heart and mind, giving me supernatural hope. Amen.

Day 21: Friday

Today, I choose to fast from the wound of *regret*.

Do you think back in time to the moment just before it all went wrong? Whatever your *it* might be, you wonder how much better your life would be if things had been different. You regret not making a different decision. You can't get that moment back, but you know things would have turned out better *if only*. We know regret has a place in our lives when we dwell on *would've*, *should've*, and *could've*. While sorrow brings us to repentance, conversion, and a deeper relationship with God, regret is a dead end, deflating replay of what went wrong. Regret keeps us focused on negative thoughts and emotions about our past. Let's allow God to convert our regret to sorrow today so that he can bring us to repentance, conversion, and freedom.

Pause to hear God speak . . .

"For godly sorrow produces a salutary repentance without regret, but worldly sorrow [regret] produces death."
—2 Corinthians 7:10

"Brothers, I for my part do not consider myself to have taken possession. Just one thing: forgetting what lies behind but straining forward to what lies ahead, I continue my pursuit toward the goal, the prize of God's upward calling, in Christ Jesus."

—Philippians 3:13–14

Take time to ask yourself . . .

What do I regret?
Why am I unwilling to let this go?

Pray slowly . . .

Heavenly Father,

In the name of our Lord Jesus Christ, I renounce regret and repent all the ways in which I have sinned because of it, particularly the ways in which I have focused on negative things. I reject regret in every area of my life. I renounce any lies that I have come to believe, including "I can never recover from that," and I renounce any companion emotions such as disappointment, worry, and hopelessness. Send your Holy Spirit to transform my heart and mind, giving me supernatural hope. Amen.

Prayer Meditation on Greed and Hopelessness

Invite God to be with you now.

Father, send your Holy Spirit to minister to the deep places of my heart during these moments of quiet reflection. Allow my own hurts, pains, and wounds to be drawn into the very wounds of Jesus that we reflect upon today. Jesus, you showed us that the way to the resurrected life is through death to the bondage of sin and wounds. Allow me to receive you, Jesus, during this time of prayer, to know that you desire to heal the pain and hurts of my heart. Lord Jesus, I trust you to guide me during this time with you. Come, Holy Spirit.

1. Quietly reflect . . .

Think of a time that you've experienced deep feelings of hopelessness. Specifically name the emotions that you are experiencing.

2. Pray . . .

Lord, I trust you to care for my heart in this time. Please show me any places within my life where these emotions are rooted (perhaps a memory).

What did God show you?

3. Write down the negative things you believe about yourself, about God, and about others in the emotions and memory.

4. If the Lord showed a memory to you, pray . . .

Lord, I thank you for exposing this painful experience and memory to me. Please reveal to me anything that you would like me to know.

In our painful memories, we often believe that God was not present to us in those difficult experiences. If we prayerfully invite the Lord into those memories, he will often reveal himself to us. As you do this, you might see an image in your mind, hear him speak to you, or just have a *sense* of him, which might be as simple as experiencing the truth come against the wrong belief in your heart, which is at the source of your pain. This simple contemplative/imaginative prayer can help us to know God in a more personal and intimate way.

If you don't experience anything in this exercise, that is OK too. Often, wounds and sins buddy up, which makes them stubborn. If that is the case, don't be discouraged! Just allow the Lord to work in his time.

5. Pray . . .

Lord, I thank you for healing grace. I trust that you speak to the deepest places of my heart even if I don't sense it. I thank you for instilling in me the truth of your deep and extravagant love for me. I thank you, as I pray right now, for restoration of every area of my life that has been stolen or compromised by sin and wounds. I bless your name!

Day 22: Saturday

Today, I choose to fast from the wound of *deferred hope*.

Are you tired of waiting for something you believed would happen? Maybe it's a promotion, a new home, or healing of some hurt or ailment. Maybe you haven't given up completely, but you have begun to wonder. You have waited so long for something that now you wait in sadness. This is deferred hope. Waiting for something good to come or happen is hard. We want our desire to be fulfilled. The longer we wait, the harder it is to hope joyfully for what we expect. Sadness creeps into our waiting. If we don't stop this sadness, it eventually kills hope altogether. Deferred hope is the foundation for hopelessness. We can end up waiting, believing in God but not in his goodness. This sadness can also move us out of waiting and into grasping for it *now*. Waiting, though, has benefits for us. It reveals our motives, builds patience, transforms our character, and builds dependency on God. Let's look for all the ways in which deferred hope has caused us to let go of dreams or to strive out of a sense of hopelessness.

Pause to hear God speak . . .

"Hope deferred makes the heart sick, but a wish ful-filled is a tree of life."

—Proverbs 13:12

"I wait for the LORD, my soul waits and I hope for his word."

—Psalm 130:5

Take time to ask yourself . . .

Do I have any dreams or desires that I have almost given up on? Why?

How do I feel when I think of the things I've almost lost hope in?

Pray slowly . . .

Heavenly Father,

In the name of our Lord Jesus Christ, I renounce deferred hope and repent all the ways in which I have sinned because of it, particularly the ways in which I have focused on negative things. I reject deferred hope in every area of my life. I renounce any lies that I have come to believe, and I renounce any companion emotions such as disappointment, worry, and hopelessness. Send your Holy Spirit to transform my heart and mind, giving me supernatural hope. Amen.

Feast Day: Sunday

Today, I choose to feast on *liberality* and *hope*.

Liberality is the virtue that replaces greed, and hope is the healing of hopelessness. By knowing that God is our ultimate provider, we are able to be generous with others and willing to help. We come to liberality by knowing that God loves us and cares for us. In today's gospel reading, Jesus heals the man who was born blind. If there was a man in Israel that had good reason to be hopeless, it was this poor blind man. Besides the disability, his blindness made him a social outcast. His entire life had been disappointing and hopeless. But Jesus calls him forward, giving the man the gift he could hardly fathom—healing of his blindness. There isn't much fanfare, just some mud and spit rubbed on the man's eyes. But Jesus does call him to a tiny response that is rooted in hope. He tells the man to "go wash in the Pool of Siloam" (Jn 9:7). The man has enough hope to *try*. Jesus didn't require much, but the action was one of faith and hope. Likewise, Jesus can do *much* with our *little*. Let's celebrate today how much God can do for us in our littleness!

Try to get to Mass a little early today. Settle into your seat, and offer your week to God. In your mind, place it on the altar and prepare your heart for the gifts of the liturgy. As you pray for the Lord's mercy during the Penitential Act, allow your heart to release greed and hopelessness.

Embrace the good news (gospel) of liberality and hope that is available to you, and celebrate your restoration and healing in the Eucharist.

Remember that Lent is the preparation for resurrection, for freedom, for joy.

Pause to hear God speak . . .

"We are the Easter people and hallelujah is our song."

—St. John Paul II

"Through whom we have gained access [by faith] to this grace in which we stand, and we boast in hope of the glory of God. Not only that, but we even boast of our afflictions, knowing that affliction produces endurance, and endurance, proven character, and proven character, hope."

—Romans 5:2–4

"But you, LORD, are a shield around me; my glory, you keep my head high. With my own voice I will call out to the LORD, and he will answer me from his holy mountain. I lie down and I fall asleep, [and] I will wake up, for the LORD sustains me. I do not fear, then, thousands of people arrayed against me on every side."

—Psalm 3:4–7

Take time to ask yourself . . .

How is God generous to me?

What are things I hope for the most?

Pray slowly . . .

Heavenly Father,

In the name of our Lord Jesus Christ, and by the power of the Holy Spirit, I accept the gifts of liberality and hope in my life. I accept my identity as the beloved child of a gracious Father God. I thank you for my life's purpose and the strength to fulfill it. I accept your healing grace. Amen.

WEEK 5. GLUTTONY AND FEAR

Day 23: Monday

Today, I choose to fast from the sin of *gluttony*.

Thanksgiving might be the day we most associate with gluttony, with its turkey, dressing, sweet potatoes, and pumpkin pie. While overeating is certainly one example of gluttony, we can really understand this sin if we think of it as *overindulgence*. Our gluttony might be related to food, but it can really involve anything that delights our senses. If we separate the pleasure of an experience from its purpose, that is probably gluttony. In ancient Rome, people would gorge themselves on food, and then force themselves to throw up so that they could eat more food. They ate only for pleasure, not for nourishment, which is its purpose. We can just as easily become spiritual gluttons. If our relationship with God focuses only on the good things we can get from him, including feelings of intimacy and closeness, that is gluttony. We focus on the sweet taste of the gift, instead of the giver. Intimacy with God is a good thing, but the purpose of our prayer is to grow in holiness.

Pause to hear God speak . . .

"Devils take great delight in fullness, and drunkenness and bodily comfort."

—St. Athanasius

"You cleanse the outside of cup and dish, but inside they are full of plunder and self-indulgence."

—Matthew 23:25

Take time to ask yourself . . .

What do I overindulge in?

What does it mean for me to grow closer to God?

Pray slowly . . .

Heavenly Father,

In the name of our Lord Jesus Christ, I renounce gluttony and repent all the ways in which I have operated in it. I reject every form of gluttony in my life. I ask you, Father, to forgive me, and I forgive myself for my gluttonous heart and actions. Holy Spirit, make me aware of any gluttonous thoughts, feelings, and actions. Amen.

Day 24: Tuesday

Today, I choose to fast from the wound of *fear*.

Our initial reactions to fear are always the same—*fight, flee,* or *freeze.* Our heart pounds inside our chest, we sweat, and we breathe rapidly. Our body and mind are on some kind of high alert to danger. If we are being stalked by a cougar while hiking in the mountains, this is the perfect response. It springs from an actual event. But when our fear is based on the *perception* that something bad *might* happen, we are experiencing the wound of fear. If you've ever been involved in a serious car accident, you probably experienced fear the first few times you got back in a car. If it became entrenched, you might experience fear every time you get in a car, even to the point of refusing to get in a car. We all have fears. Yours might be public speaking, death, or poverty. Our fears often become ingrained because of hurtful or traumatic events. Fear can keep us from living God's plan for us. We either rush ahead of God (fight), run away (flee), or stand still (freeze). I encourage you to take heart as we continue this reflection over the coming days. Fear will try to stop you. Do not be deterred!

Pause to hear God speak . . .

"I command you: be strong and steadfast! Do not fear nor be dismayed, for the LORD, your God, is with you wherever you go."

—Joshua 1:9

"Even though I walk through the valley of the shadow of death, I will fear no evil, for you are with me; your rod and your staff comfort me."

—Psalm 23:4

Take time to ask yourself . . .

What is going on in my life when I experience fear? How do I react when I feel afraid?

Pray slowly . . .

Heavenly Father,

In the name of our Lord Jesus Christ, I renounce fear and repent all the ways in which I have sinned because of it, particularly the ways in which I have not trusted you in the midst of my fear. I reject every form of fear in my life. I renounce any lies that I have come to believe, including lies such as "Bad things happen to me," "I cannot trust others," or "I'm vulnerable." I renounce any companion emotions such as doubt, mistrust, and unbelief. Send your Holy Spirit to speak the truth to my heart that I am protected, cared for, and loved. Amen.

Day 25: Wednesday

Today, I choose to fast from the wound of *doubt*.

If fear were a building, doubt would probably be the foundation on which it was built. We tend to treat doubt casually. The phrase *I doubt that* is commonplace. There are all kinds of board and card games where doubt is an important strategy. But we should not be confused—doubt is a danger to our lives. It may come to us as a simple thought that makes us feel a little bit *off*. The thought may be something such as "What if I'm wrong?" or "What if I make a mistake?" Before long, though, doubt has reduced us to fearful uncertainty. When we recognize doubt, and don't allow it to take us to fear, though, it will propel us closer to God. St. Thomas told the other disciples that he would have to see the risen Jesus before he believed. But he did not allow his doubt to force him back to his old life out of fear. Instead, he brought his doubt to Jesus, where it was transformed in an incredible encounter with the

Lord. As we continue our meditation today, let's follow Thomas's example to go to the other side of doubt.

Pause to hear God speak . . .

"For God did not give us a spirit of cowardice but rather of power and love and self-control."

—2 Timothy 1:7

Then [Jesus] said to Thomas, "Put your finger here and see my hands, and bring your hand and put it into my side, and do not be unbelieving, but believe."

—John 20:27

Take time to ask yourself . . .

What causes me to doubt in my life?
How do I doubt myself? How do I doubt God?

Pray slowly . . .

Heavenly Father,

In the name of our Lord Jesus Christ, I renounce doubt and repent all the ways in which I have sinned because of it, particularly the ways in which I have doubted you and opened the door to fear. I reject doubt in every area of my life. I renounce any lies that I have come to believe, including lies such as "I'll make a mistake" or "I'll be wrong." I renounce any companion emotions such as fear, mistrust, and unbelief. Send your Holy Spirit to speak the truth to my heart that I am filled with the gift of faith. Amen.

Day 26: Thursday

Today, I choose to fast from the wound of *unbelief*.

You can always check your level of unbelief with a simple question: *Am I focused on my problems or his promises?* Belief activates God's grace in our lives. Unbelief pulls us into a downward spiral. Our problems look insurmountable, and the solutions are nowhere in sight. When Moses sent twelve spies into the land of Canaan, ten saw giants, while only Caleb and Joshua saw the promise of the land of milk and honey. Joshua had seen God deliver Israel from Egypt and many miracles in the desert. Joshua believed that God was bigger than giants. When we don't experience God in a powerful and supernatural way, unbelief has an easier way into our lives. God becomes an ideology or distant being. Unbelief turns us back to our former misery (like the Israelites wanting to return to slavery in Egypt) instead of forward into the promise of God! As we reflect today, let us focus on God's promise in the midst of our problems.

Pause to hear God speak . . .

"'But if you can do anything, have compassion on us and help us.' Jesus said to him, '"If you can!" Everything is possible to one who has faith.' Then the boy's father cried out, 'I do believe, help my unbelief!'"

—Mark 9:22–24

"The father realized that just at that time Jesus had said to him, 'Your son will live,' and he and his whole household came to believe."

—John 4:53

Take time to ask yourself . . .

What part of my life seems to have more problems than promise?

What are the giants in my life?

Pray slowly . . .

Heavenly Father,

In the name of our Lord Jesus Christ, I renounce unbelief and repent all the ways in which I have sinned because of it, particularly the ways in which I have seen problems instead of promise, wanted to go back to old things, and thought poorly of you. I reject every form of unbelief in my life. I renounce any lies that I have come to believe, including lies such as "God won't come through" or "Miracles are for others." I renounce any companion emotions such as fear, doubt, and mistrust. Send your Holy Spirit to bring me into the promise, power, and goodness you have planned for me. Amen.

Day 27: Friday

Today, I choose to fast from the wound of *mistrust*.

We trust people every day without giving it a second thought—other drivers, airline pilots, or the mechanic who fixed our brakes. Yet when we are hurt by those we know, we might stop trusting them. Sometimes that is wisdom. But we can also allow our hurts to influence the way we live our daily lives. We stop trusting and begin to live cautiously. We expect that others will disappoint us and that they are not reliable. If you've ever found yourself thinking, "I knew it would end badly. I always thought they'd eventually hurt me," mistrust probably has a place within your heart. We often mistrust God, too. If you think that he is smaller than your circumstances or that he isn't near—that is mistrust. Because of our mistrust, we withhold or pull back in order to protect ourselves. Especially on this Friday, let's allow Jesus to meet us in our mistrust.

Pause to hear God speak . . .

"If God so clothes the grass of the field, which grows today and is thrown into the oven tomorrow, will he not much more provide for you, O you of little faith?"

—Matthew 6:30

"Trust in the LORD with all your heart, on your own intelligence do not rely."

—Proverbs 3:5

Take time to ask yourself . . .

What relationship do I *not* trust? Why?
With what part of my life do I not trust God? Why?

Pray slowly . . .

Heavenly Father,

In the name of our Lord Jesus Christ, I renounce mistrust and repent all the ways in which I have sinned because of it, particularly the ways in which I have relied on my own understanding and sabotaged relationships. I reject mistrust in every area of my life. I renounce any lies that I have come to believe, including lies such as "Everybody will eventually disappoint me" or "Miracles are for others." I renounce any companion emotions such as fear, doubt, and unbelief. Send your Holy Spirit to bring me into the promise, power, and goodness you have planned for me. Amen.

Prayer Meditation on Gluttony and Fear

Invite God to be with you now.

Father, send your Holy Spirit to minister to the deep places of my heart during these moments of quiet reflection. Allow my own hurts, pains, and wounds to be drawn into the very wounds of Jesus that we reflect upon today. Jesus, you showed us that the way to the resurrected life is through death to the bondage of the world. Allow me to receive you, Jesus, during this time of prayer, to know that you desire to heal the pain and hurts of my heart. Lord Jesus, I trust you to guide me during this time with you. Come, Holy Spirit.

1. Quietly reflect . . .

Think of a time that you've experienced deep feelings of fear. Specifically name the emotions that you are experiencing.

2. Pray . . .

Lord, I trust you to care for my heart in this time. Please show me any places within my life where these emotions are rooted (perhaps a memory).

What did God show you?

3. Write down the negative things you believe about yourself, about God, and about others in the emotions and memory.

4. If the Lord showed a memory to you, pray . . .

Lord, I thank you for exposing this painful experience and memory to me. Please reveal to me anything that you would like me to know.

In our painful memories, we often believe that God was not present to us in those difficult experiences. If we prayerfully invite the Lord into those memories, he will often reveal himself to us. As you do this, you might see an image in your mind, hear him speak to you, or just have a *sense* of him, which might be as simple as experiencing the truth come against the wrong belief in your heart, which is at the source of your pain. This simple contemplative/imaginative prayer can help us to know God in a more personal and intimate way.

If you don't experience anything in this exercise, that is OK too. Often, wounds and sins buddy up, which makes them stubborn. If that is the case, don't be discouraged! Just allow the Lord to work in his time.

5. Pray . . .

Lord, I thank you for healing grace. I trust that you speak to the deepest places of my heart, even if I don't sense it. I thank you for instilling in me the truth of your deep and extravagant love for me. I thank you, as I pray right now, for restoration of every area of my life that has been stolen or compromised by sin and wounds. I bless your name!

Day 28: Saturday

Today, I choose to fast from the wound of *insecurity*.

I was boarding a flight once, listening to the *beep, beep, beep* of the travelers in front of me as their boarding passes were scanned. Suddenly, there was a harsh, dissonant tone. It was an invalid boarding pass. The poor offending passenger had mixed up his boarding passes. You could see his panic and fear at that moment as the security of his travel plans was cast into doubt. Insecurity is a form of fear that tells us we are not good enough, that we are not accepted or embraced. We believe that we are not welcome and secure in a hostile world. We see ourselves as incapable, inadequate, and unacceptable. Just as an invalid boarding pass keeps us off an airplane, our beliefs and emotions that are rooted in insecurity keep us out of life. Insecurity causes us to shrink from challenging situations or to overcompensate and strive. As you reflect on insecurity today, be attentive to your thoughts, feelings, and beliefs.

Pause to hear God speak . . .

"Now, if you obey me completely and keep my covenant, you will be my treasured possession among all peoples, though all the earth is mine."

—Exodus 19:5

"For those who are led by the Spirit of God are children of God. For you did not receive a spirit of slavery to fall back into fear, but you received a spirit of adoption, through which we cry, 'Abba, Father!' The Spirit itself bears witness with our spirit that we are children of God."

—Romans 8:14–16

Take time to ask yourself . . .

What do I believe about myself and others when I feel like I don't belong?
How do I react when I feel insecure?

Pray slowly . . .

Heavenly Father,

In the name of our Lord Jesus Christ, I renounce insecurity and repent all the ways in which I have sinned because of it. I reject insecurity in every area of my life. I renounce any lies that I have come to believe, including lies such as "I'm not safe" or "I'm not adequate." Send your Holy Spirit to heal, restore, and transform me. I belong to you. I am loved by you. I am chosen by you. I am known to you. Amen.

Feast Day: Sunday

Today, I choose to feast on *abstinence* and *safety/security*.

Abstinence is the virtue that replaces gluttony, and safety/security is the healing of fear. By keeping our focus on the giver of every gift rather on the gifts that he provides, we are able to grow in abstinence. In today's gospel reading, Jesus shows us that no gift is beyond him, including the supernatural gift of life. Mary and Martha have sent word to Jesus that Lazarus is dying. But Jesus isn't in any particular rush to return to Bethany to heal Lazarus.

When Jesus finally arrives, Martha says to him, "Lord, if you had been here, my brother would not have died" (Jn 11:21). She is focused on the gift and not the giver. Jesus is the giver, and every gift is within his power. Even as Jesus commands the tomb to be opened, Martha warns that Lazarus's body will smell. But upon seeing the supernatural power of Jesus, she comes to believe and to trust.

Try to get to Mass a little early today. Settle into your seat, and offer your week to God. In your mind, place it on the altar and prepare your heart for the gifts of the liturgy. As you pray for the Lord's mercy during the Penitential Act, allow your heart to release gluttony and fear.

Embrace the good news (gospel) of abstinence and safety/security that is available to you, and celebrate your restoration and healing in the Eucharist.

Remember that Lent is the preparation for resurrection, for freedom, for joy.

Pause to hear God speak . . .

"We are the Easter people and hallelujah is our song."
—St. John Paul II

"Even though I walk through the valley of the shadow of death, I will fear no evil, for you are with me; your rod and your staff comfort me. You set a table before me in front of my enemies; you anoint my head with oil; my cup overflows. Indeed, goodness and mercy will pursue me all the days of my life; I will dwell in the house of the LORD for endless days."

—Psalm 23:4–6

"I give them eternal life, and they shall never perish. No one can take them out of my hand. My Father, who has given them to me, is greater than all, and no one can take them out of the Father's hand."

—John 10:28–29

Take time to ask yourself . . .

How am I secure in Jesus?

What are some ways I can focus on God as giver?

Pray slowly . . .

Heavenly Father,

In the name of our Lord Jesus Christ, and by the power of the Holy Spirit, I accept the gifts of abstinence and security/safety in my life. I accept my identity as the beloved child of a gracious Father God. I thank you for my life's purpose and the strength to fulfill it. I accept your healing grace. Amen.

WEEK 6. ANGER AND REJECTION

Day 29: Monday

Today, I choose to fast from the sin of *anger*.

If you've ever been really angry, you probably wondered to yourself after you settled down, "Who was that person?" Your anger left you physically, emotionally, and mentally exhausted. If you turned that anger outward, you probably damaged relationships. Anger is a devastating sin in our lives. Think of sinful anger as a wild animal. It has sharp claws and vicious teeth, and it wants to destroy everything around it while destroying itself in the process. Oftentimes, we get angry when we feel out of control—we learn that we can control those around us with our anger. As we will see during this week, the sin of anger connects powerfully to the wound of rejection, although it can also connect to feelings of powerlessness and fear. Whether our anger is outward (rage, violence, abuse) or more subtle (passive-aggressive), it is damaging to ourselves and those around us. Let's have the courage today to look honestly at our anger and bring it to God.

Pause to hear God speak . . .

"This deadly cancer of anger . . . makes us unlike ourselves, makes us like timber wolves or furies from Hell, drives us forth headlong upon the points of swords, makes us blindly run forth after other men's destruction as we hasten toward our own ruin."

—St. Thomas More

"Do not let anger upset your spirit, for anger lodges in the bosom of a fool."

—Ecclesiastes 7:9

Take time to ask yourself . . .

What kinds of things make me angry?
When I am angry, what am I feeling? Rejection? Powerlessness? Fear?

Pray slowly . . .

Heavenly Father,

In the name of our Lord Jesus Christ, I renounce anger and repent all the ways I have sinned because of it. I reject every form of anger in my life. I ask you, Father, to forgive me, and I forgive myself for my angry heart and actions. Holy Spirit, make me aware of any angry thoughts, feelings, and actions. Amen.

Day 30: Tuesday

Today, I choose to fast from the sin of *bitterness*.

When you eat a bitter food, it often leaves a sour look on your face. Emotional bitterness has the same effect on our insides. It poisons our hearts and gives life an "unpalatable" taste. We can be bitter toward others as well as toward ourselves. In both cases, bitterness has one outcome—destruction. If we are routinely sarcastic, harsh, and hostile, we should check for bitterness. If we constantly criticize the failings or shortcomings of ourselves or others, bitterness probably has a hold in our lives. The scriptures refer to bitterness as a root, meaning that it is unseen. When we allow bitterness to take root in our lives, we often blame those around us for our circumstances, rather than take responsibility for the way we handle them. As we reflect today, let's expose this bitter root.

Pause to hear God speak . . .

"Love alone makes heavy burdens light and bears in equal balance things pleasing and displeasing. Love bears a heavy burden and does not feel it, and love makes bitter things tasteful and sweet."

—Thomas à Kempis

"See to it that no one be deprived of the grace of God, that no bitter root spring up and cause trouble, through which many may become defiled."

—Hebrews 12:15

Take time to ask yourself . . .

Who am I bitter toward (sarcastic, hostile, harsh)?
What in my life has feelings of bitterness attached to it?

Pray slowly . . .

Heavenly Father,

In the name of our Lord Jesus Christ, I renounce bitterness in my life and repent all the ways I have sinned because of it. I reject every form of bitterness in my life. I ask you, Father, to forgive me, and I forgive myself for my bitter heart and actions. Holy Spirit, make me aware of any bitter thoughts, feelings, and actions. Amen.

Day 31: Wednesday

Today, I choose to fast from the sin of *resentment.*

Think of resentment as firewood for your anger. The intensity of anger needs fuel to keep it burning hard. Resentment is that fuel! When we remain indignant at unfair treatment, and hold a grudge, we are resentful. We are unable to let go of a wrong that we think has been done to us. Anger will subside if it is not fueled by resentment. But resentment dwells on injustice and unfairness. On the inside, we feel unsettled in our heart and our soul. Sometimes our resentment is based on real injustice, but other times it stems from our *perception* that someone treated us unfairly. The solution for resentment is simple—forgiveness. St. Augustine is sometimes credited for saying, "Resentment is like drinking poison and expecting the other person to die."

Pause to hear God speak . . .

"Resentment . . . is rejection of God."

—St. Ignatius Brianchaninov

"Does a spring gush forth from the same opening both pure and brackish water?"

—James 3:11

Take time to ask yourself . . .

Whom do I resent?
Do I hold a grudge against anyone?

Pray slowly . . .

Heavenly Father,

In the name of our Lord Jesus Christ, I renounce resentment in my life and repent all the ways I have sinned because of it. I reject every form of resentment in my life. I ask you, Father, to forgive me, and I forgive myself for my resentful heart and actions. Holy Spirit, make me aware of any resentful thoughts, feelings, and actions. Amen.

Day 32: Thursday

Today, I choose to fast from the sin of *unforgiveness*.

If resentment is firewood for your anger, unforgiveness is gasoline! Especially when we've been deeply hurt, we think that forgiveness means letting the other person off the hook, as though what happened to us was OK. Forgiveness, though, isn't about the other person. Forgiveness is about *us*. Unforgiveness actually keeps us tied to our hurt. Unforgiveness has been medically linked to early death, arthritis, cancer, heart disease, and a number of other physical ailments. Forgiveness is easier than we think, since it is a decision, not a feeling. In fact, when we *decide* to forgive, our emotions will eventually follow our decision. There are four important keys to forgiveness:

1. Decide to forgive—don't wait for your emotions.
2. Depend on God—grace is the antidote for negative emotions.
3. Pray for the other person.

4. Bless them—speak well of the other person and
    don't gossip.

As we reflect today, let's have the courage to forgive
those who have wronged us.

Pause to hear God speak . . .

"'Should you not have had pity on your fellow servant,
as I had pity on you?' Then in anger his master hand-
ed him over to the torturers until he should pay back
the whole debt. So will my heavenly Father do to you,
unless each of you forgives his brother from his heart."

—Matthew 18:33–35

"All bitterness, fury, anger, shouting, and reviling must
be removed from you, along with all malice. [And] be
kind to one another, compassionate, forgiving one
another as God has forgiven you in Christ."

—Ephesians 4:31–32

Take time to ask yourself . . .

Who in my past or present have I not forgiven?
What benefit do I think I get by holding on to
unforgiveness?

Pray slowly . . .

Heavenly Father,

In the name of our Lord Jesus Christ, I renounce unforgiveness and repent all the ways I have sinned because of it. I reject every form of unforgiveness in my life. I ask you, Father, to forgive me, and I forgive myself for my unforgiving heart and actions. Holy Spirit, make me aware of any unforgiving thoughts, feelings, and actions. Amen.

Day 33: Friday

Today, I choose to fast from the wound of *rejection*.

Has anyone ever said something to you that made you feel like you weren't wanted or needed? You might have felt as if you were left out or shunned. All of these emotions are typical of rejection. Wounds of rejection are very common among children who have experienced death, divorce, or other traumatic separations. Even in adults, deep rejection can negatively affect our identity (thoughts and beliefs about ourselves). Rejection is a wound of *belonging*. We believe that we don't belong! If rejection lives in our hearts, it can bear destructive fruit in our lives, including unforgiveness, hard-heartedness, and resentment. We will also misunderstand an important part of God's mercy. Oftentimes, man's rejection is God's protection!

Pause to hear God speak . . .

"Be content with what you have, for he has said, 'I will never forsake you or abandon you.'"

—Hebrews 13:5

"He came to what was his own, but his own people did not accept [rejected] him."

—John 1:11

Take time to ask yourself . . .

When have I experienced rejection?

What do I believe about myself when someone rejects me?

Pray slowly . . .

Heavenly Father,

In the name of our Lord Jesus Christ, I renounce rejection and repent all the ways in which I have sinned because of it. I reject this wound in every area of my life. I renounce any lies that I have come to believe, including lies such as "I do not belong" or "I am unwanted." Send your Holy Spirit to heal, restore, and transform me. I belong to you. I am loved by you. I am chosen by you. I am known to you. Amen.

Prayer Meditation on Anger and Rejection

Invite God to be with you now.

Father, send your Holy Spirit to minister to the deep places of my heart during these moments of quiet reflection. Allow my own hurts, pains, and wounds to be drawn into the very wounds of Jesus that we reflect upon today. Jesus, you showed us that the way to the resurrected life is through death to the bondage of the world. Allow me to receive you, Jesus, during this time of prayer, to know that you desire to heal the pain and hurts of my heart. Lord Jesus, I trust you to guide me during this time with you. Come, Holy Spirit.

1. Quietly reflect . . .

Think of a time that you've experienced deep feelings of rejection or anger. Specifically name the emotions that you are experiencing.

2. Pray . . .

Lord, I trust you to care for my heart in this time. Please show me any places within my life where these emotions are rooted (perhaps a memory).

What did God show you?

3. Write down the negative things you believe about yourself, about God, and about others in the emotions and memory.

4. If the Lord showed a memory to you, pray . . .

Lord, I thank you for exposing this painful experience and memory to me. Please reveal to me anything that you would like me to know.

In our painful memories, we often believe that God was not present to us in those difficult experiences. If we prayerfully invite the Lord into those memories, he will often reveal himself to us. As you do this, you might see an image in your mind, hear him speak to you, or just have a *sense* of him, which might be as simple as experiencing the truth come against the wrong belief in your heart, which is at the source of your pain. This simple contemplative/imaginative prayer can help us to know God in a more personal and intimate way.

If you don't experience anything in this exercise, that is OK too. Often, wounds and sins buddy up, which makes them stubborn. If that is the case, don't be discouraged! Just allow the Lord to work in his time.

5. Pray . . .

Lord, I thank you for healing grace. I trust that you speak to the deepest places of my heart, even if I don't sense it. I thank you for instilling in me the truth of your deep and extravagant love for me. I thank you, as I pray right now, for restoration of every area of my life that has been stolen or compromised by sin and wounds. I bless your name!

Day 34: Saturday

Today, I choose to fast from the wound of *control/manipulation*.

When you were a baby and realized that someone would respond to your cries, you discovered your ability to influence your world. As we grow, we learn more and more sophisticated ways of influencing the world around us. The wound of control/manipulation is a distorted way to influence our world. We don't behave based on mutual goodness. Instead, we operate with our own safety as the primary concern. Our control and manipulation make our world more predictable and *safe*. But others see us as *using* or *taking advantage* of them. We might work very hard to manage circumstances behind the scenes and artfully influence people against their own will. As we go through the rest of this reflection, let's be especially aware of the people and circumstances we manipulate or control.

Pause to hear God speak . . .

"Finally, draw your strength from the Lord and from his mighty power."

—Ephesians 6:10

"I am the vine, you are the branches. Whoever remains in me and I in him will bear much fruit, because without me you can do nothing."

—John 15:5

Take time to ask yourself . . .

How do I control/manipulate others to get them to do what I want?

What happens if I don't control?

Pray slowly . . .

Heavenly Father,

In the name of our Lord Jesus Christ, I renounce control/manipulation and repent all the ways in which I have sinned because of them. I reject control/manipulation in every area of my life. I renounce any lies that I have come to believe, including lies such as "I'm out of control; I'm not safe." Send your Holy Spirit to heal, restore, and transform me. I belong to you. I am loved by you. I am chosen by you. I am known to you. Amen.

Feast Day: Sunday

Today, I choose to feast on *patience* and *acceptance*.

While our anger often produces immediate results, those outcomes are often not what we'd like—and they come at the price of infecting our relationships with bitterness, resentment, and unforgiveness. Patience, though, actually produces the outcomes that we really hope for. It replaces anger and builds a sense of belonging and acceptance. Today's gospel represents the entry into Holy Week, and in it we can clearly see these truths unfold. The chief priests and Pharisees, tired of being embarrassed by this Jesus character, have moved in their anger to have him killed. They mock, insult, and lie in order to rid themselves of Jesus. In doing so, they reject the One they claim to worship. Jesus, though, patiently accepts the circumstance, embarrassment, and humiliation of the moment. He wants what the Father wants— redemption for the world. He is confident in who he is, confident in his Father, and confident in his mission.

Try to get to Mass a little early today. Settle into your seat, and offer your week to God. In your mind, place it on the altar and prepare your heart for the gifts of the liturgy. As you pray for the Lord's mercy during the Penitential Act, allow your heart to release anger and rejection.

Embrace the good news (gospel) of patience and acceptance that is available to you, and celebrate your restoration and healing in the Eucharist.

Remember that Lent is the preparation for resurrection, for freedom, for joy.

Pause to hear God speak . . .

"We are the Easter people and hallelujah is our song."

—St. John Paul II

"But if we hope for what we do not see, we wait with endurance."

—Romans 8:25

"And, like living stones, let yourselves be built into a spiritual house to be a holy priesthood to offer spiritual sacrifices acceptable to God through Jesus Christ."

—1 Peter 2:5

Take time to ask yourself . . .

What are some ways I would like to be accepted?

What types of things make me impatient?

Pray slowly . . .

Heavenly Father,

In the name of our Lord Jesus Christ, and by the power of the Holy Spirit, I accept the gifts of patience and acceptance in my life. I accept my identity as the beloved child of a gracious Father God. I thank you for my life's purpose and the strength to fulfill it. I accept your healing grace. Amen.

WEEK 7. LUST AND POWERLESSNESS

Day 35: Monday

Today, I choose to fast from the sin of *lust*.

We've made it to the last week of Lent! Your diligence has paid off. As we enter this holiest week of the Church year, let's gather up some zeal and uproot the last deadly sin on our list—lust. We usually think of lust in terms of sexual desire. But if we expand our thinking just a bit, we can really understand how deadly this sin is. Lust, like gluttony, is an attachment to pleasures of the flesh. With lust, though, the pleasure we get comes at the expense of other people. We take something from them that doesn't belong to us. Pornography, masturbation, and sexual fantasy violate the dignity of others, turning their bodies, or our own, into *things*. Lust isn't just a sin of action but a sin of our thoughts. As we reflect today, may God bring us to conversion from any lust in our lives.

Pause to hear God speak . . .

"Passing encounters are only a caricature of love; they injure hearts and mock God's plan."

—St. John Paul II

"But I say to you, everyone who looks at a woman with lust has already committed adultery with her in his heart."

—Matthew 5:28

Take time to ask yourself . . .

Where in my life do I serve myself over others?
How do I use others to get the things that I want?

Pray slowly . . .

Heavenly Father,

In the name of our Lord Jesus Christ, I renounce lust and repent all the ways in which I have sinned because of it. I reject every form of lust in my life. I ask you, Father, to forgive me, and I forgive myself for my lustful heart and actions. Holy Spirit, make me aware of any lustful thoughts, feelings, and actions. Amen.

Day 36: Tuesday

Today, I choose to fast from the wound of *powerlessness*.

We've all experienced it: being in a situation that we couldn't anticipate, didn't want, and couldn't escape. Maybe it was the death of a loved one, a cancer diagnosis, or being physically abused. It is true that many things happen in our lives that are beyond our control. However, sometimes we attempt to gain worldly strength and control over our feelings of weakness and vulnerability. Instead of trusting God with our difficult circumstance, we feel overwhelmed or believe that there is no way out. So we try to gain power ourselves. As we begin to trust God more deeply, we can resist the temptation to use our bodies or the bodies of others to gain false power. As we ponder this Holy Week, let us remember that the power of Jesus' Resurrection into glory was a result of the powerlessness of his flesh.

Pause to hear God speak . . .

"I am the vine, you are the branches. Whoever remains in me and I in him will bear much fruit, because without me you can do nothing."

—John 15:5

"'My grace is sufficient for you, for power is made perfect in weakness.' I will rather boast most gladly of my weaknesses, in order that the power of Christ may dwell with me."

—2 Corinthians 12:9

Take time to ask yourself . . .

When do I feel powerless or overwhelmed?
What do I believe about myself or my situation when I feel powerless?

Pray slowly . . .

Heavenly Father,

In the name of our Lord Jesus Christ, I renounce powerlessness and repent all the ways in which I have sinned because of it. I reject powerlessness in every area of my life. I renounce any lies that I have come to believe, including lies such as "I am overwhelmed,"

"I'm trapped," or "I don't know what to do." Send your Holy Spirit to transform me and give me the full measure of Christ's strength in the midst of my weakness. I belong to you. I am loved by you. I am chosen by you. I am known to you. Amen.

Day 37: Wednesday

Today, I choose to fast from the wound of *weariness*.

Have you felt weary before? Not just tired but completely exhausted of your strength, vigor, energy, and stamina? Weariness occurs when we overexert our mind, will, body, soul, and spirit. Weariness happens when there is more of us in something than is good for us. We push and push and push until there is nothing left in us. Weariness is the sad outcome of attempting to exert our own power.

Our weariness can open the door to despair and disappointment. After all, we've invested far more than we should, and still we haven't reached our goal. Even holy people can be afflicted by weariness. If you find yourself weary, there are a few simple tools to help break its grip on you:

1. Refresh with a change of pace or time away.
2. Connect with others.

3. Refocus on God's perspective about what is important.

Let's allow God to minister to our weariness as we continue the reflection today.

Pause to hear God speak . . .

"Come to me, all you who labor and are burdened, and I will give you rest. Take my yoke upon you and learn from me, for I am meek and humble of heart; and you will find rest for yourselves. For my yoke is easy, and my burden light."

—Matthew 11:28–30

"Unless the Lord build the house, they labor in vain who build. Unless the Lord guard the city, in vain does the guard keep watch. It is vain for you to rise early and put off your rest at night, to eat bread earned by hard toil—all this God gives to his beloved in sleep."

—Psalm 127:1–2

Take time to ask yourself . . .

What types of activities make me weary?
Where in my life do I feel overburdened?

Pray slowly . . .

Heavenly Father,

In the name of our Lord Jesus Christ, I renounce weariness and repent all the ways in which I have sinned because of it. I reject weariness in every area of my life. I renounce any lies that I have come to believe, including lies such as "I just don't have the strength" or "It's too much." Send your Holy Spirit to heal, restore, and transform me. I belong to you. I am loved by you. I am chosen by you. I am known to you. Amen.

Day 38: Thursday

Today, I choose to fast from the wound of *self-pity*.

Sometimes, through no fault of our own, we are the victim of the harshness of life. Many other times, we have some measure of responsibility for our circumstance. In either case, when we begin to demand sympathy from everybody around us, self-pity is probably at work in us. We may exaggerate and indulge ourselves in our own pain. As a result, we excuse ourselves from the daily struggle that is the Christian life. Our words or thoughts might be, "It's too much for me to deal with," "This is so hard," or "My struggle is just too great." One of self-pity's ugliest qualities is that it ignores the obvious needs of others. We read in the scriptures that the prophet Jonah fell into deep self-pity when the gourd plant that provided him shade died. He was so consumed with himself that he forgot the 120,000 people in the city of Nineveh. Let's look for this destructive wound today and remove it from our lives.

Pause to hear God speak . . .

"Then the LORD said, 'You are concerned over the gourd plant which cost you no effort and which you did not grow; it came up in one night and in one night it perished. And should I not be concerned over the great city of Nineveh, in which there are more than a hundred and twenty thousand persons who cannot know their right hand from their left . . . ?'"

—Jonah 4:10–11

Take time to ask yourself . . .

What in my life do I demand that people have sympathy for?
When do I get lost in my own difficulty to the point that I lose sight of the pain of those around me?

Pray slowly . . .

Heavenly Father,

In the name of our Lord Jesus Christ, I renounce self-pity and repent all the ways in which I have sinned because of it. I reject self-pity in every area of my life. I renounce any lies that I have come to believe, including lies such as "This is just too much" or "My life is harder than everybody else's." Send your Holy Spirit to heal, restore, and transform me. I belong to you. I am loved by you. I am chosen by you. I am known to you. Amen.

Day 39: Friday

Today, I choose to fast from the wound of *self-neglect*.

Do you constantly put yourself at the end of the line—physically, emotionally, and spiritually? Neglecting our own well-being is one of the ways that we keep ourselves powerless. We trap ourselves inside mottos such as *God first, family second, others third, self last*. While it is true that we become our best self in giving ourselves to others, we can twist this into a kind of powerlessness, rather than a free gift of self. Jesus freely chose to go to the Cross, to lay down his life for us. He chose to set aside rightful power and strength. In self-neglect, we wear ourselves out to justify and excuse our own feelings of powerlessness. We say to ourselves, "You have to wait," "Everybody else ahead of you," or "You can't decide for yourself." Jesus chose, out of the fullness of who he was, to make a gift of himself.

Pause to hear God speak . . .

"But seek first the kingdom [of God] and his righteous-ness, and all these things will be given you besides."

—Matthew 6:33

"I am the vine, you are the branches. Whoever remains in me and I in him will bear much fruit, because with-out me you can do nothing. . . . If you remain in me and my words remain in you, ask for whatever you want and it will be done for you. By this is my Father glori-fied, that you bear much fruit and become my disciples. As the Father loves me, so I also love you. Remain in my love."

—John 15:5, 7–9

Take time to ask yourself . . .

What part of my life (spiritual, emotional, physical) do I tend to neglect?

Do I give myself to others from the greatness of who God has made me to be or as a way of allowing myself to be powerless?

Pray slowly . . .

Heavenly Father,

In the name of our Lord Jesus Christ, I renounce self-neglect, and repent all the ways in which I have sinned because of it. I reject self-neglect in every area of my life. I renounce any lies that I have come to believe, including lies such as "I always have to be last" or "I'll always be exhausted." Send your Holy Spirit to heal, restore, and transform me. I belong to you. I am loved by you. I am chosen by you. I am known to you. Amen.

Prayer Meditation on Lust and Powerlessness

Invite God to be with you now.

Father, send your Holy Spirit to minister to the deep places of my heart during these moments of quiet reflection. Allow my own hurts, pains, and wounds to be drawn into the very wounds of Jesus that we reflect upon today. Jesus, you showed us that the way to the resurrected life is through death to the bondage of the world. Allow me to receive you, Jesus, during this time of prayer, to know that you desire to heal the pain and hurts of my heart. Lord Jesus, I trust you to guide me during this time with you. Come, Holy Spirit.

1. Quietly reflect . . .

Think of a time that you've experienced deep feelings of lust or powerlessness. Specifically name the emotions that you are experiencing.

2. Pray . . .

Lord, I trust you to care for my heart in this time. Please show me any places within my life where these emotions are rooted (perhaps a memory).

What did God show you?

3. Write down the negative things you believe about yourself, about God, and about others in the emotions and memory.

4. If the Lord showed a memory to you, pray . . .

Lord, I thank you for exposing this painful experience and memory to me. Please reveal to me anything that you would like me to know.

In our painful memories, we often believe that God was not present to us in those difficult experiences. If we prayerfully invite the Lord into those memories, he will often reveal himself to us. As you do this, you might see an image in your mind, hear him speak to you, or just have a *sense* of him, which might be as simple as experiencing the truth come against the wrong belief in your heart, which is at the source of your pain. This simple contemplative/imaginative prayer can help us to know God in a more personal and intimate way.

If you don't experience anything in this exercise, that is OK too. Often, wounds and sins buddy up, which makes them stubborn. If that is the case, don't be discouraged! Just allow the Lord to work in his time.

5. Pray . . .

Lord, I thank you for healing grace. I trust that you speak to the deepest places of my heart, even if I don't sense it. I thank you for instilling in me the truth of your deep and extravagant love for me. I thank you, as I pray right now, for restoration of every area of my life that has been stolen or compromised by sin and wounds. I bless your name!

Day 40: Saturday

Today is our final lenten reflection.

My hope is that this fast becomes a way of life for you. What we have done over the last forty days is to fast from the things in our life that move us away from God and away from our true happiness. Like a drug addict, we receive momentary relief from pain when we live in our sins and wounds but no freedom and no resurrection life.

Most of us would like to have resurrection. Yet we shy away from the Cross, which is the only way to get to that resurrection. On this final day of fasting, take everything that you have uncovered in the last forty days to the Cross—sins, wounds, hurts, and painful memories. Take some extra time to ask God to speak to the things that are most broken in your life. Allow God to heal and restore what has been broken or stolen from your life. My prayer is that you will have the courage to crucify everything in your life that is not God.

Pause to hear God speak . . .

"Is this not, rather, the fast that I choose: releasing those bound unjustly, untying the thongs of the yoke; setting free the oppressed, breaking off every yoke? . . . Then your light shall break forth like the dawn, and your wound shall quickly be healed; your vindication shall go before you, and the glory of the LORD shall be your rear guard."

—Isaiah 58:6, 8

Take time to ask yourself . . .

What sin or wound do I most need to release to God? What causes me to resist?

Pray slowly . . .

In the name of our Lord Jesus Christ, I crucify the sin of sloth.

In the name of our Lord Jesus Christ, I crucify the sin of pride.

In the name of our Lord Jesus Christ, I crucify the sin of envy.

In the name of our Lord Jesus Christ, I crucify the sin of greed.

In the name of our Lord Jesus Christ, I crucify the sin of gluttony.

In the name of our Lord Jesus Christ, I crucify the sin of anger.

In the name of our Lord Jesus Christ, I crucify the sin of lust.

Jesus, I renounce confusion and place it before your feet at the Cross.

Jesus, I renounce abandonment and place it before your feet at the Cross.

Jesus, I renounce shame and place it before your feet at the Cross.

Jesus, I renounce hopelessness and place it before your feet at the Cross.

Jesus, I renounce fear and place it before your feet at the Cross.

Jesus, I renounce rejection and place it before your feet at the Cross.

Jesus, I renounce powerlessness and place it before your feet at the Cross.

Amen.

Feast Day: Easter Sunday

Today, I choose to feast on *chastity* and *empowerment*.

Maybe you think about chastity in terms of sexual purity. Chastity is really about saying yes to God's plan for our body and our identity. We come to chastity by knowing who we are in God's eyes rather than our own eyes or the eyes of others. Today's gospel represents *the* turning point in all of human history. It's on this day that Jesus fulfills his own yes to the Father. With his Resurrection, Jesus moves from anointing to glory. Jesus has redeemed every sin—sloth, pride, envy, greed, gluttony, anger, and lust. And he has healed every wound—confusion, abandonment, shame, hopelessness, fear, rejection, and powerlessness.

Today, we share in the Easter joy. Over these last forty days, you may have pressed more deeply into the dark corners of your life than ever before. You've probably confronted some pain and hurt. Hopefully, you've received the healing mercy of God as you've faithfully sought freedom. If you are still struggling, I encourage you to take heart. Even in your pain, God continues to work. He desires good for you. Lean on him. Surrender yourself to him. Invite him in.

I encourage you to attend the Easter Vigil Mass tonight. Settle into your seat, and offer your entire Lenten fast to God. In your mind, place it on the altar and prepare your heart for the gifts of the liturgy. As you pray for the Lord's mercy during the Penitential Act, allow your heart to release all your sins and wounds.

Embrace the good news (gospel) of virtue and healing that is available to you, and celebrate your own resurrection into the glory of who God has created you to be!

Pause to hear God speak . . .

"We are the Easter people and hallelujah is our song."

—St. John Paul II

"The glory of God is man fully alive."

—St. Irenaeus

"Blessed be the God and Father of our Lord Jesus Christ, who in his great mercy gave us a new birth to a living hope through the resurrection of Jesus Christ from the dead, to an inheritance that is imperishable, undefiled, and unfading, kept in heaven for you."

—1 Peter 1:3–4

Take time to ask yourself . . .

What healing and freedom have I experienced this Lent?

What healing and freedom do I still desire?

Pray slowly . . .

Heavenly Father,

In the name of our Lord Jesus Christ, and by the power of the Holy Spirit, I accept the gifts of diligence and understanding, humility and connectedness, kindness and worthiness, liberality and hope, abstinence and security, patience and acceptance, and chastity and empowerment in my life. I accept my identity as the beloved child of a gracious Father God. I thank you for my life's purpose and the strength to fulfill it. I accept your healing grace. Amen.

Ken Kniepmann is a Catholic speaker, writer and former executive director of the John Paul II Healing Center in Tallahassee, Florida, where he remains serving in a variety of organizational and ministry capacities. His extensive ministry experience includes teaching apologetics and serving as a retreat leader and youth ministry volunteer.

Kniepmann served on the board of directors of the John Paul II Center and at Capital City High School, Return to Glory Ministries, and FRATERNUS. He earned a bachelor's degree in psychology and a master's degree in counselor education from St. Louis University. He blogs for *Catholic Stand*.

He and his wife, Sharon, live in Tallahassee with their children.

Bob Schuchts is the bestselling author of *Be Healed* and *Be Transformed* and founder of the John Paul II Healing Center in Tallahassee, Florida.

AVE

Founded in 1865, Ave Maria Press,
a ministry of the Congregation of
Holy Cross, is a Catholic publishing
company that serves the spiritual and
formative needs of the Church and its
schools, institutions, and ministers;
Christian individuals and families; and
others seeking spiritual nourishment.

For a complete listing of titles from

Ave Maria Press

Sorin Books

Forest of Peace

vi

D0003036

AVE MARIA PRESS
Notre Dame, IN
A Ministry of the United States Province of Holy Cross